MUSIC AT THE EDGE

Through the words of the therapist and the words and music of the client, *Music at the Edge* allows the reader to experience a complete music therapy journey. Francis, a musician living with AIDS, challenged Colin Lee, the music therapist, to clarify his feelings about living and dying within the therapeutic process. In doing so he helped the therapist to discover aspects of this particularly demanding form of therapeutic work and to question the framework of the therapeutic relationship in palliative care.

Music at the Edge is a complete music therapy case study. After an introduction outlining the practice of music therapy in palliative care, the author relates Francis's particular history. There are two types of music incorporated in this project: notational examples in the text, to give an indication of the intricacies of the musical content to readers and musicians, and the enclosed CD containing extracts from the sessions themselves.

The CD is a central part of the book, allowing readers to *hear* extracts from Francis's improvisations which illuminate the text and provide the musical 'voice' of the client. These extracts are a unique insight into the therapeutic process when working with death and dying. Transcribed music allows all those able to read music to follow and play selections from Francis's improvisations.

This unusual and very moving book offers anyone who is working with, or facing, illness and death an opportunity to understand how the transcendent power of music can enable expression of feelings more accurately than words.

Colin Lee is a music therapist working in palliative care and in postgraduate education.

D0962658

MUSIC AT THE EDGE

The music therapy experiences of a musician
with AIDS

Colin Lee

London and New York

First published 1996
by Routledge
11 New Fetter Lane, London EC4P 4EE

Simultaneously published in the USA and Canada
by Routledge
29 West 35th Street, New York, NY 10001

Routledge is an International Thomson Publishing Company

© 1996 Colin Lee

Typeset in Monophoto Times by
Datix International Limited, Bungay, Suffolk

Printed and bound in Great Britain by
Clays Ltd, St Ives PLC

British Library Cataloguing in Publication Data

A catalogue record for this book is available from the British Library

Library of Congress Cataloguing in Publication Data
Lee, Colin
Music at the edge : music therapy experiences of a musician with AIDS / Colin Lee.
Includes bibliographical references (p. 163) and index.
1. Music therapy – Case studies.   2. AIDS (Disease) – Palliative treatment.
3. AIDS (disease) – Case studies.   I. Title.
ML3920.L42   1996
616.97'92065154 – dc20   95–25782

ISBN 0–415–12463–8
0–415–12464–6 (pbk)

CONTENTS

FIGURES

CD EXTRACTS

FOREWORD

Because this book's central concern is the power of immediacy in creating music for therapy it is, and will always be, utterly contemporary. Unique in all its aspects, it is an enthralling biography in two voices: the one, Francis, a gifted pianist of middle age with AIDS, determined to realize his life in musical expression to the fullest possible extent; the other, Colin Lee, a sensitive music therapist, whose courageous initiative in accommodating his client's pressing needs sets the circumstances for an extraordinary disclosure of music creation's therapeutic potency. The book is also a testament expressed through dual media: music and words. The consistent recording of the client and therapist's sessions enables the availability of their improvised music on compact disc, and words in print. Excerpts of the music that was the life-flow of their relationship can be relived in the context of their transcribed discussions.

In a unique synthesis of original music and searching commentary, Francis lives and expresses his processes of discovery. We can follow his deepening release into musical freedom, his amazement and joy in creative achievement, his piloting journey of reconciliation and transformation toward the inevitability of death. Because he ardently *lives* his process, realizes it in and through music improvisation, and articulates it with astounding clarity, we are led into recognizing, at first hand, the therapeutic essence of creative involvement in making music. There is nothing of intellectual conceit in his statements, nothing of extraneous theory, just the clear perceptive exegesis of experience – in which everything is intrinsic to music. The therapist, his constant companion on an inspiring, disquieting journey into the unknown, empirically tends, reflects and augments each step in the process. On the recordings his playing is in creative resonance with his client's; his voice in the text offers a counterpoint that serves to place their work in the larger context of music therapy practice.

Everything about this book is of interest to music therapists: the many aspects of music it discusses – improvisation and composition, keys and scales, tonality and atonality, structure and expression, creative freedom and constraints, chaos and organization, silences, improvisational devices –

are all subject to consideration from a practical orientation toward music-making for therapy.

As Colin Lee narrates Francis's and his journey, he diverges to consider at length, connect and amplify, the artistic and professional themes that arise. Addressing the personal vulnerability of the therapist, he makes no attempt to hide the stress he was under, or the confusion he often felt when faced with the strength of his client's presence and demands. He describes the anguish of being so deeply involved in the dying process of an intensely living man, and intimates that it is necessary for therapists who are creative artists to acknowledge that the very nature of their work and sensitivities predisposes them to hurt and distress, anxiety and uncertainty.

Inevitably, the book traces the progressive nature of the illness, and the deterioration of Francis's physical condition. We accompany the changes in his inner life and are stirred by his searching considerations of human values and needs. Remarkably, and in ways that are both poignant and liberating, as his health worsened, so the breadth and depth of his involvement in creative music therapy became unbounded. His thoughts on music itself, its powers of expression, and its potential as therapy became ever more lucid; his statements, often of considerable poetic beauty, always carry the authenticity of direct experience. In his commentaries he provides insights into the dynamics of music therapy that can only come from a client – and from a client suffering as he did, while possessing the skills, insight and command of language to formulate his perceptions. Because he so totally lived his course of therapy, made himself his own subject of research, and ultimately proposes that his music and descriptions of his experiences be publicly disseminated, he becomes an eloquent, convincing teacher.

The strands of the book interweave around the central experience of its music. Through the recorded excerpts we have the privilege of sharing in the experiential groundwork of the course of therapy, stage by stage. Is it because these improvisations are so saturated in the immediacy of expression that the quality of our listening has the capacity to dissolve the separation between our here and now, and the there and then of their playing? The immediacy of creative expression renders the intervening chasms of time illusionary, seeming to leap easily into the now, bringing us into intimate contact with the living presence of the musician. We hear and feel his state of mind with a cogency that words cannot communicate. Yet we need the words: the book's intelligent and heartfelt discussions serve to complement our musical impressions and frame them in an interpretive understanding that leads us deeper into the mysteries that invest humankind with musical life. And this in turn, of course, enhances our listening.

Music at the Edge is indeed a landmark book for music therapists, for all who work in healing services, for all musicians and for all who cherish music. Even more, it is a profound testament to the integrity and indomitable potential of the human spirit. It touches on everyone's life.

Dr Clive Robbins
Co-Director,
The Nordoff-Robbins Center For Music Therapy,
New York University, 1995

ACKNOWLEDGEMENTS

First, I would like to remember Francis. He is owed the greatest debt, as without his words and music this book would not exist. I hope, had he been alive, he would have been pleased with the outcome. His painstaking attention to detail was a constant reminder that accuracy of reflection is an essential part of valid assessment. His flights of creativity, musically and verbally, are the very fibre of the book. If there is one lesson I learnt from our time together it is that life, art and music therapy cannot be permanent. One must search for new avenues of expression; art that reaches a plateau cannot, in essence, be creative.

London Lighthouse, where I worked one day a week for three years during my research, was supportive at many levels. They provided one of the most enviable rooms in which to work and placed great value on music therapy as part of the complementary therapies programme. Thank you to my counsellors Aileen and Patti; I could not have continued without their sensitive guidance. Being a part of such a visionary organization was a constant inspiration, and during my time there I gained a philosophy of living and dying that continues to influence my life and work. City University also played a large part in my life during this time, providing me with an opportunity to expand through teaching and performing as well as to consider the intricacies of practice and research. I must also thank the Oxford Music Therapy Charity and the Nordoff-Robbins Music Therapy Center, without whose financial assistance this project would not have been possible.

To my research supervisors, Leslie Bunt and Eric Clarke, I owe a great debt for it was they who helped me organize my often irrational thinking. Since then other colleagues have been influential. Thanks to Kenneth Bruscia, who gave me much advice in the early stages and helped focus the original vision, and to the anonymous reader who aided in shaping the final structure of the book; to Andrea Gilroy, who was always there to listen, criticize and support, and to Cathy Brady and Diana Hayter who helped with editing the manuscript. My close friends always extended a listening ear, suffering many repetitions of my constant insecurities and doubts. Thanks also to my supervisor and mentor Rachel Wheeler-Robinson. Her clinical clarity influenced my writing at many levels. Special thanks to Clive Robbins who painstakingly checked and helped illuminate the final manuscript. His belief and foresight were crucial in the final stages of the book. Our time in New York will remain with me always.

Finally I would like to extend gratitude to Sir Michael Sobell House Hospice, where I now work, for providing the impetus to complete the book. The constant support I received has been an inspiration. To Patricia, Dianne, Ann, Carrie, Carolyn, Rosalind, Hazel, Rosemary and all the staff, patients and volunteers in day-care. Thank you for believing.

The author and publisher would like to thank the following for permission to reproduce material published elsewhere: on p. 22 an extract from *Music Therapy in Palliative/Hospice Care* by Susan Munro published by MMB Music, Inc.; on p. 77 an extract from *The Musical Life* by Walter Matthieu reprinted by arrangement with Shambhala Publications, Inc., Boston; on p. 104 an extract from 'Writing with Light' by Douglas Dunn appearing in *Elegies*, published by Faber & Faber Ltd.; on p. 130 an extract from *The Chasm of Fire* by Irina Tweedie published by Element Books of Shaftesbury, Dorset; an extract from *Chroma* by Derek Jarman by permission of the Estate of the author and Random House UK Ltd. Every effort has been made to obtain permission to reproduce copyright material throughout this book. If any proper acknowledgement has not been made the copyright holder should contact the publishers.

For Robin

1

BACKGROUND

INTRODUCTION

This book describes an extraordinary flight in music therapy with Francis, a musician who lived with and died of AIDS. It will trace the re-awakening of his creative musical spirit, which, through earlier circumstances, had been lost. Francis and I explored many regions as client and therapist during the last year of his life; this story is a testament to his journey towards death. The structure of the book is formed around his course of therapy, his music, and his words transcribed session by session. In the context of the narration, I also describe my involvement in the therapy process: my searchings and reflections, and the professional and personal challenges this extraordinary experience of 'therapy in music' brought into my life. The selection of excerpts of music from the sessional recordings on the accompanying compact disc enables the reader to share in the creative and expressive dynamics of Francis's journey. With regard to the transcriptions of his words: apart from determining punctuation, and some slight editing in the interests of clarity, the words are as he spoke them. The immediacy of improvisation through speech, as well as music, is retained.

The book is essentially non-academic: all theoretical constructs, apart from those presented in Chapters 2 and 11, appear naturally as the text unfolds. The reader, uninitiated in this area of practice, whether layman, musician, health-care professional or student, will be able to comprehend the content fully, with little or no previous knowledge of music therapy.

The motivation for producing this book came from two sources. First a promise. A promise made to Francis before he died that our work together would be documented and presented for publication. I remember clearly when the subject was first broached during the last days of his life. After he had planted the initial seed we immediately began to speculate on matters of language and style. My mind soared as our conversation became more and more enlivened by the possibilities we envisioned. At the same time, I began to feel a sense of uncertainty as I realized the significance of what he was entrusting to me. I nervously made a commitment to realize our vision; the content and format Francis put in my hands. It has often felt a heavy burden, keeping our relationship alive for longer than at times felt comfortable. However, I never regretted our pledge: the objective appraisal of our work demanded by the writing, enabled me to explore and clarify many principles central to music therapy with people living with terminal illnesses.

Secondly, I saw the opportunity for a description of music therapy in which the verbal and musical voices of client and therapist combine to express the essence of the process. Music therapists normally evaluate their work from their own frame of reference; the understanding gained comes from the therapist's descriptions and interpretations. Inevitably, many clients, owing to the extent of their mental or physical dysfunctions, are unable to provide articulate verbal responses. This has always been a problem in assessing the effectiveness of music therapy. With the widening of music therapy practice into areas where clear verbal evaluations are forthcoming it is essential that therapists learn to consider attentively what the client is saying. Advancements in electronic technology have made high-quality audio recordings of sessions easily attainable. With the client's permission, the music that has been therapeutic can itself be preserved for documentation, and through assessment and research disclose and demonstrate the inherent components and dynamics of the process.

BEGINNINGS

In order to give a backdrop to the content of this book, I must first retrace some of my steps as a music therapist. The opportunity to work in the field of HIV and AIDS came when I gained the Research Fellowship in Music Therapy at City University, London in 1988. Until then I had worked with children and adults who had learning disabilities, at first in a special school, then later in a large hospital complex. Initiating and developing a new department within the hospital took time, dedication and commitment. I devoted many hours to meetings, putting forward arguments for music therapy both in the hospital and in the development of community care. To present the case clearly it was necessary to provide succinct presentations of the work to an often uninformed and sceptical management audience. After five years I had secured a department encompassing learning disabilities and mental health which employed three qualified staff and two helpers.

During my last year at the hospital I became increasingly interested in the potential role of music with dying people. My curiosity stemmed from reading the small amount of literature available on the subject (Bailey 1983, Munro 1978, 1984). The hospital had a small unit for clients who were physically ill, known as the Hospital Ward, which was apart from the main community. Clients were referred for many reasons, from the common cold through to post-operative and palliative care. At first I had not thought to include this ward within the music therapy programme. Certainly, I had never

2

heard of a client with a learning disability being referred to music therapy specifically because of a palliative condition. Reflecting on the literature, I could see no way of adapting the approaches described to the needs of my developmentally disabled clients. Neither I nor any of the music therapy team had undertaken music therapy with such very ill people. What little contact there had been had come through therapists visiting clients with whom they had worked, which was felt to be a humanistic extension of the relationship, rather than a time for formally scheduled sessions. We rarely continued music therapy in these circumstances for the simple reason that we mistakenly considered the clients to be too ill to respond.

After months of deliberation and self-questioning I set up a programme that provided the option of taking direct referrals from the Hospital Ward. This decision was made with considerable trepidation, for death and dying were on the periphery of my clinical experience. Although only a few clients in the hospital had died, the experiences had always been disturbing, and had left me with many unanswered questions. I felt confusion and pain in response to loss. On consideration, I began to understand that I was blocking the intrinsic meaning of endings by denying their impact on the music therapy process: it would be essential for me to face this issue if I were to continue growing as a music therapist.

What was I hoping to answer within myself by facing this potentially difficult work? Many powerful therapeutic encounters occurred during the following months. Questions and doubts found their level as I allowed myself the vulnerability of working with the unknown. As the programme developed, the Hospital Ward took more of my time physically and emotionally. My concern was now much less with the patient's learning disabilities and more with the effects of the presenting physical illness. The music therapy sessions were nearly always ward-based, requiring me to take a digital piano and a selection of percussion instruments to the bedside. This new sphere of work involved an immediacy I had not encountered before. The therapeutic processes of working in the context of multiple disabilities seemed to gather momentum when a person was chronically sick or dying. Clients would often express what I felt to be intense mirrors of inner anguish: there was pain in their eyes; I sensed the increased confusion in their minds. They could neither understand nor articulate what was happening to them. In therapy there were periods of extended musical simplicity and silence that somehow looked beyond the boundaries I had so carefully built in my practice. Questions surfaced: What was I doing? How could my professional imperative to formulate aims relate to people in the last stages of life?

The sudden death of a long-term client acted as a catalyst in motivating me to approach our two local hospices with a view to offering music therapy to their patients. My initial contacts were uneasy as neither hospice felt music therapy to be a priority. Their medical staffs could conceive of music as relaxation or diversion but felt uncomfortable about introducing what they saw as the potentially explosive dynamics of improvisation in music therapy. They were worried that this form of expression would be too unsettling or intrusive when a person was very ill or dying. After many frustrating talks and meetings our negotiations broke down. The proposal for the Research Fellowship at City University was my final attempt to set up work in this area.

I chose to focus my research on people living with HIV and AIDS for various reasons. Practically I wanted to limit my proposal to one specific area of palliative care. HIV and AIDS was an issue of great public concern at the time and seemed the most natural area to choose. Apart from pragmatic considerations, other more personal motives soon arose. I do not intend to expound on these here. Some will become clear as the book unfolds, others are too intimate to include. I felt the reaction of society to the emergence of HIV and AIDS to be both shocking and apocalyptic. As publicity gained momentum I remember being struck by the hysteria of scaremongering, and the effects this might have on a person living with the virus. Perhaps music therapy could play a role in ameliorating the stress experienced in living with HIV and AIDS? How could music therapy accompany the dying process? What effect might musical expression have on the progression of the virus itself? These questions felt more like hypotheses. They were wide-ranging and pointed toward the potential connection between creativity in music and the personal dynamics of living with a terminal illness. To this day I have kept them alive.

LONDON LIGHTHOUSE

London Lighthouse, a centre facing the challenge of AIDS, was the first facility to offer me a placement for the research. Lighthouse is Britain's first major residential and support centre for people living with HIV and AIDS. The centre is committed to providing the best possible care so that people affected by AIDS can live – in all the senses this word embraces. Lighthouse felt genuine; it was the first organization to welcome the idea of including the creative arts within its complementary therapies programme. I felt that the innovatory nature of Lighthouse's history (Cantacuzino 1993) supplemented my need for creative freedom as a music therapist. I began working there one day a week soon after it had opened in January 1989. There was much to be learnt both in terms of music therapy practice and the evaluation that would need to be undertaken in the research. My work with critically ill people took place on the residential unit, on the top floor of the building. The beautiful Ian McKellan hall was allotted to me for sessions with clients who were asymptomatic. By the end of the first six months I had acquired, by donation, a grand piano with an extensive range of percussion instruments (see Figure 1).

Working at London Lighthouse was an experience tinged with excitement and apprehension. Lighthouse is a unique and visionary organization, its

4

Figure 1 The Music Therapy Room, Ian McKellan Hall, London Lighthouse

central philosophy based on the unconditional acceptance of every human spirit. Together with this is the attitude that death and dying are to be accepted as belonging to life. These values strongly affected my work as a music therapist. From the beginning I had to explore my own finiteness. I had been working at Lighthouse for one year before I met Francis. During this time I had begun the often painful journey of addressing my own fears of death and dying, the consequences of which greatly influenced my ensuing work. Without this in-depth analysis it would not have been possible for me to work with clients' needs and fears either musically or verbally. After seven years of working with the dying I am still travelling this road.

One reason for wanting to work within the field of HIV and AIDS was my abhorrence of the persecution of minority groups. At Lighthouse I could embrace my philosophy that every person is a unique presence regardless of past choices, and that music therapy is about acceptance and growth. I wanted to offer room in which people could explore their inner world without condition or pressure. One opportunity to do this came with a client who wanted me to play the piano while he sang love songs about another man. He explained that he was unable to find anyone who was prepared to take on such an accompanying role. The request was simple and one I gladly undertook. I believe it allowed him the opportunity to express his true feelings of tenderness as a gay man. We worked together for six months exploring songs by George Gershwin and Cole Porter, and singing present-day ballads. For me this highlighted the need for music therapy to be totally open to the idiosyncratic needs of every person.

The sessions at Lighthouse were often vastly different from my expectations. Until now improvisation had formed the main core of my therapeutic practice. Faced with situations that previously had been outside my experience, I had to become more versatile. Listening with clients to CDs, playing pre-composed music and developing solely verbal relationships, were all avenues that were new to me. While improvisation was still my main therapeutic modality it became clear that I would need to be flexible in accommodating alternative, but equally important, music therapy approaches. I found myself constantly having to reconsider my therapeutic boundaries. By letting go of previous ideas and allowing uncharted situations to become an essential part of my work I began to make sense of the ever-changing challenges to therapy practice.

Through experience and counselling I began to understand that to be effective as a music therapist working with clients with HIV and AIDS, I would need to evolve a different and more critical sense of honesty both in music itself and in the therapeutic relationship. This was particularly apparent during improvisations. I wondered whether it would be possible to maintain such musical closeness in every therapeutic situation. The initial work at Lighthouse pointed toward a concept that I now consider to be fundamental for a music therapist in palliative care – that music therapy allows expressions of health and life as well as endings, death and dying. In essence the justification for this book is that it emphasizes Francis's *life* in the context of his approaching death. The most striking paradox in expressing music while living with a terminal diagnosis is that as a person's physical life shrinks and dies, more often than not their music grows and becomes stronger. This core of musical representation and dying represents, I believe, the true inner nature of music-making within palliative care. Beginnings and endings, life and death, interpenetrate and conjoin to form the apex of the therapeutic relationship and ensuing creative music therapy processes.

FRANCIS

In recalling my initial reactions to Francis, I remember being immediately struck by his presence and his age. I was accustomed to meeting people at Lighthouse who were my contemporaries, yet here was a middle-aged man who could have easily been my father, and who carried himself elegantly, his long grey hair held back in a ponytail. There was a fastidious quality about the way he dressed that commanded respect.

The year spent at Lighthouse before our meeting had been difficult, for working with clients of a similar age raises emotions that remain personally challenging. The sense of suffering for a peer group holds a special depth of intensity. Dass and Gorman (1985, p. 77) suggest that:

> Our hearts go out to these people, not only because of the immediate circumstances but because, intuitively, we recognize the response of mental suffering that we ourselves would experience under such conditions. Their predicament awakens our own fears and pain of loss of control.

The journey Francis and I were to undertake was one that would change both our lives. Music therapy granted him a completely different way of addressing the last year of his life. It allowed him time to reflect on his past and future, particularly providing time for re-evaluation of the significance he placed on his perceived lack of successful relationships: he was estranged from his family and had never experienced a lasting personal relationship. Music therapy opened doors to worlds that never ceased to amaze him. I remember the dramatic impact when he discovered he could, after much apprehension, improvise, and how directly music could express his feelings. He often came to sessions anxious because he felt he had reached such heights during the preceding improvisations that there could be nothing more to follow. His fears were, however, always unfounded, the therapeutic direction of our work becoming clearer and more refined as time progressed. It was as if there were no limits to the musical pastures through which he could forage. As his illness became more acute so his improvisations became more sophisticated and less dependent on such previous musical influences as

7

Liszt, Debussy, Prokofiev and others. By freeing himself from the styles of established composers, Francis found a beauty of expression that was a direct reflection of his own emotions. His concern with musical aesthetics was replaced by a personal expression that displayed an intensity in every note he played.

For me, our time together was one of constant exploration. It is undeniable that music therapists encounter certain critical clients with whom they feel a special affinity. This gives rise to relationships that are dynamic or musically powerful, and which provide opportunities for professional growth and learning. On a personal level we meet clients to whom we are spontaneously drawn. Just as good friendships develop naturally, certain clients become close. Acknowledging such special relationships is fundamental for growth and understanding of the therapeutic process. Francis presented me with the challenge of reappraising areas of professionalism in ways that changed my understandings of music therapy, endings and life. The regions we examined were often unexplored for us both, repeatedly causing apprehension for Francis as voyager, and uncertainty for me in my role as therapist. In overcoming these difficulties, the eventual outcome was one of clarity for us both. He taught me how little music therapists understand about the dynamics of improvisation and how important musical components are in achieving the balance between therapy and art that is essential for the perception of the creative. I faced his approaching death with great heaviness, at times consciously disregarding that our time was limited. Our sessions became so much part of my life that it was difficult to imagine not having the weekly human adventure of working to meet his musical and therapeutic needs. His eventual death, together with my own grief, acted as an anchor in assessing the time we had spent together. I freely mourned the passing of a fellow-spirit with an intensity I had not experienced before, and rarely since.

STRUCTURE OF THE BOOK

The text

The text presents the therapeutic process comprehensively, and incorporates Francis's evaluations alongside my own assessments. Chapter 2 presents theoretical and philosophical foundations, providing an academic substructure. This is included as an orientational review rather than a formal academic survey and is not essential to an understanding of the main narrative. The book then proceeds to present the thoughts and feelings of client and therapist in a therapeutic context. At the beginning of each chapter, a review of the central issues discusses how they affected my role within the sessions, through the counselling I received, and in the subsequent direction of our work. The main emphasis is not to place the therapeutic process within a theoretical framework but rather to give a full description of what happened and how the dynamics changed Francis, the process and myself. Any development of theories, excluding those raised in chapters 2 and 11, originates from within the narrative. Chapter 10 recounts the time from when Francis became too ill to participate up until his death. It addresses what happens in a music therapy relationship with a dying person, when the music itself and the maintenance of therapeutic boundaries become inappropriate. Francis's physical deterioration required the development of a new relationship: we became friends. I describe the last days of his life and their importance for us both. Facing the imminence of his death was a necessary final stage as we approached the dissolving of the unique relationship that had changed both of our lives; my reflections on this period have been painful to articulate. Chapter 11 attempts to bring together certain strands of the book, as well as drawing some philosophical and theoretical conclusions from the text as a whole. It leads into a coda consisting of a statement by Francis that I have entitled 'On the Creative'. With this, his voice concludes the book.

Throughout the description of sessions in chapters 2 to 10, interpretation has been kept to a minimum. My reflective comments during and at the end of each chapter are questions as much as theoretical conclusions. Psychotherapeutic impressions are not inferred. This is not to say that a psychotherapeutic exploration of our relationship would not have been possible. Indeed, I hope the implicit connections between the content of the sessions and various traditional approaches to music therapy will become evident. Francis and I felt it important to differentiate the origins of our work, embedded as it was in clinically realized musical constructs and creative inspiration, from current but musically extrinsic psychotherapeutic theories and practice. That being said, much of the content is conveyed through verbal explorations and the written word. Francis's insightful comments on the music therapy process and his interpretations of music constitute one of the book's most powerful statements. He could never have denied the importance of verbal language, but was always clear that his journey and expression came foremost through music. He asked that I write freely and honestly about our experiences; complying with this request has not always been an easy task. Because of the complications in translating often new and profound ideas into words, descriptions vary in implication. None of my observations are intended as judgements; but it is impossible in life always to be impartial, even with the best of intentions. Our therapeutic journey was a partnership, and I have tried to reflect this throughout the writing. I have tried to be loyal to my memories, allowing Francis's presence to live in my mind, imagining what he would have said were he alive. The freedom of structure in the writing hopefully parallels the musical autobiography he achieved at its most profound and spiritual level.

The Music

Music is presented in two ways in the text: notational examples which indicate the intricacies of musical content; and the accompanying compact disc, which forms a central part of the book as it provides the opportunity to hear extracts from the sessions. This musical illumination of the text adds a fundamental dimension to the understanding of the therapeutic process. The CD can be heard with the narrative, either concurrently with the text, or freely as an extension of the written word. The text that accompanies each recorded illustration outlines its predominant features and progress. This format provides the option to hear an extract before reading, unbiased so to speak, or to read the outline before listening. Whichever way one chooses, the music will communicate the essence of the therapeutic process. Descriptions of sessions are written in the past tense, while descriptions of the music are in the present tense to reinforce the sense of its immediacy.

All examples are of piano music. In descriptions of the two piano-duets (extract one, session one, and extract three, session three) I have identified who was playing treble and who bass, so as to differentiate the musical roles. While it is important to acknowledge the musical dialogue between players, it is equally important to experience the music as itself. In listening to the example of a duet for two pianos (extract six, session nine) it is impossible to identify the differing thematic strands of the players; the important experience here lies in their therapeutic convergence. The remainder of the musical examples are piano solos by Francis. Complying with the necessary limitations of publishing, the extracts have been chosen to highlight the essential stages of the therapeutic process. I would urge the reader to listen to the music both as an expression of a therapeutic relationship but also as music in its own right. Transcriptions of Francis's commentaries and searchings are virtually complete.

CONCLUDING COMMENTS

The preparation and writing of this book has influenced and changed many of my views on music therapy. With the provision of integral audio examples in the published accounts and evaluations of music therapy (Ansdell 1995, Nordoff and Robbins 1977), the use of words becomes to some extent subsidiary. By including the music in actuality – the hard-core data, as it were – it is possible to present a much more comprehensive impression of the dynamics of music therapy. That we now have this mode of dissemination available will change how music therapy is perceived and even how, in the future, it will be developed. The experiential context itself of music therapy is now accessible for research and insight.

My impermanence as a person and professional were tested and explored throughout our work and the writing of the book. Francis was my most needing client as well as my most articulate teacher. The risk I have taken in exposing many of my deepest feelings is balanced against my fervent belief that we must recognize that therapists are human beings too. The balance between music and words, like the therapeutic relationship itself, changed and transformed as the writing progressed. I have tried to include a sense of improvisation in the structure of the writing that would mirror the musical dynamics of our sessions at their most fundamental level.

This book, then, attempts to describe a music therapy relationship with clarity and artistic objectivity. The failures and successes, unions and dissolutions, are all given equal weight in the narrative. It is my hope that the reader may gain insight into the life and content of our relationship, and grasp some of the extraordinary dynamics disclosed in the process of creative musical exploration. The story throughout bears tribute to Francis's courage, candour and visionary love for music.

2

IMPROVISATION, MUSIC THERAPY AND AIDS

> The challenge: bring order to the whole.
> Through design.
> Composition.
> Tension.
> Balance.
> Light.
> And harmony.
>
> > (Sondheim 1984.
> > *Sunday in the Park with George*)

INTRODUCTION

This chapter will provide philosophical and theoretical perspectives, and begin with a review of the literature on improvisation, questioning the apparent disparity between improvisation as art and as therapy. Concerning this I will put forward a definition of the improvisational perspectives of music therapy. Further discussions will provide a context for my views on the therapeutic effects of music. A summary of music therapy in palliative care will be related to the importance of improvisation when working with clients with HIV and AIDS.

ASPECTS OF IMPROVISATION

Etymologically, 'improvisation' is derived from the Latin past participle 'improvisus', meaning that which has not been foreseen (Durant 1984). Modern definitions are expansive and indeterminate:

> Improvisation is the art of thinking and performing music simultaneously.
>
> > (Bloom 1961)

> Improvisation is performance according to the inventive whim of the moment.
>
> > (Kennedy 1980)

Nattiez (1990), adopting a semiological viewpoint, described the basic aspects of improvisation as being 'the simultaneous performing and inventing of a new musical fact with respect to a previous performance' (p. 88), while Solomon (1986) defined improvisation as 'the discovery and invention of original music spontaneously, while performing it, without preconceived formulation, scoring or context' (pp. 16–19). Bailey (1992) perceived improvisation as requiring no argument or justification, and concluded that 'it exists because it meets the creative appetite that is a natural part of being a performing musician and because it invites complete involvement, to a degree otherwise unobtainable, in the act of music-making' (p. 142). It is interesting that the concept of the act of 'performance' is a central connecting factor. Performance is described as an 'accomplishment' (Watson 1976), though when attributed to music it becomes more particularly concerned with the previously rehearsed production of Western classical music (Levinson 1990).

Bailey (1992) further proposed that improvisation is about moving from one point to another within a space that needs to be filled. Maya (1992) described improvisation as ' . . . a state of mind. It's simply what you hear and do at the moment', and Hosinger (1992) remarked that 'you think about something, you see something and then you operate, you have the flash, like an abstract picture, and then you present it' (pp. 18–21). While these latter descriptions may seem inexplicit, they provide a more open perspective on the dynamics of improvisation. With the emergence of 'completely free improvisation', 'collective improvisation' and 'spontaneous music' in the late 1960s and early 1970s, improvisation became more flexible. Artists such as Parker, Bailey, Riley, AMM and Taylor broke the barriers between jazz and classical music with improvisations that had no preconceived or pre-thought structures. These developments were parallelled with the work of peer composers such as Stockhausen, Cage, Cardew and Boulez, whose innovations influenced all aspects of contemporary music.

Pressing (1984) explained the processes in improvisation as containing 'seeds' which are held together by a set of 'event clusters'. His study of improvisation proposed that there are two structural ideas, 'feedback' and 'feedforward', and suggested that ideas are developed from core inventions which may be 'repeated, developed or discarded'. Feedback is concerned with error correction, while feedforward looks to future events, providing a balanced structure of decision-making and design. Zinn (1981) argues that improvisation concerns skill and accomplishment. He explains that to reach a stage of competence the improviser requires years of practice. Bailey (1992), on the other hand, found that when he introduced non-musicians into his group of trained musicians the improvisations took on new dimensions. He noted that non-improvisers soon became acclimatized to the musical dynamics, finding a balance of dialogue that complemented and enhanced the improvisational direction of the whole.

The connections with music therapy are relevant. Most clients have limited musical knowledge, as distinct from therapists who, in Zinn's terms, will have spent considerable time developing their improvisational resources. This imbalance in expertise, while perhaps establishing the characteristic therapeutic roles in improvisation, often provides a forum for equality of content. A therapist must allow the skills of the client to find their level within the overall musical structure. I have experienced situations in which a client without trained skills has produced music equal in content to that of the therapist. The inborn musical abilities within everyone are the growth points for creative equality. It is this potential symmetry that forms the fundamental background for the evolution of the music therapy relationship.

Durant (1984) emphasized the interpersonal relationships of improvisers as being equal in importance to the resulting artistic production. 'Problems' and 'solutions' evolve; what for one player may be a problem, for another may not. Exploring musical and subjective models in improvisation, he investigates human relationships and conflict in terms of the dynamic interplay between improvisers (his argument loses validity, however, when he attempts to categorize improvisation as being essentially a pleasing experience). The interaction arising from the players and their personal issues, rather than the music itself, is a facet that now concerns some present-day improvisers. Prevost (1984) proposes that improvised music is self-definable; it exists because there is no other adequate form in which to express humanity. Hosinger (1992) reinforces this view: 'It seems to me to be important in a sociopolitical way, regarding how we feel about the times we live in.' Berendt (1985) argues that 'the improviser listens – firstly – to the people improvising with him, to his fellow human beings. The composer is alone. The improviser is part of the community' (p. 176). Finally, Dean (1989) discusses personal character but fails to find a balance between expression and what he terms the 'improviser's attitude to the audience'. I believe that it is the particular constellation of expectations and needs in an audience that allows only certain aspects of individual discovery to be expressed.

In the United States and the United Kingdom, the initial writings on improvisation in music therapy (Alvin 1975, Nordoff and Robbins 1965, 1971, 1977, Priestley 1975) detailed three distinct models: Creative Music Therapy (Nordoff and Robbins), Free Improvisation Therapy (Alvin) and Analytical Music Therapy (Priestley), as defined by Bruscia (1987) in his international survey of improvisational music therapy practice. This comprehensive text includes a summary of over twenty-five approaches. The comparative examination of the components defined and the final summary that attempts to find commonalties of clinical techniques makes this an influential book. It was a constant guide throughout my research and continues to provide a dependable base on which to assess new areas of improvisational practice. More recently Bunt (1994) places emphasis on improvisation as a complex, yet standard clinical technique. Ansdell (1995) considers creative music therapy with adult clients through theoretical questioning and case-studies. This is the first publication describing current applications of the Nordoff-Robbins approach to various adult populations. In concert with my own philosophical approach to improvisation in music therapy, Ansdell makes a plea that we consider musical constructs as essential to our understanding. Completed and ongoing work and research projects that consider various aspects of improvisation in music therapy (Gilroy and Lee, eds, 1995, Heal and Wigram, eds, 1993, Payne, ed., 1993) are now widely available.

It is interesting that references to improvisation in music therapy do not appear in the literature of musicology, composition or performance. The only mention of any connection between improvisation as art and as therapy appears in Durant (1984) who, in discussing the human involvement in improvisation as an aspect of musical 'production' suggests it may be 'even therapeutic'! The writings on improvisation by musicologists and music therapists barely mention each other's existence. Why is this? Perhaps the root of the problem lies in the fact that the aim of improvisation in music therapy is not to produce art, nor is it normally undertaken with an audience. Music therapists certainly attempt to produce music of artistic quality, though ultimately the musical outcome is influenced by their clients' offerings (Bruscia 1987). This means that the improvisation can be as simple or complex, as consonant or discordant, as the therapeutic direction dictates. However, as documented throughout Francis's journey, the aesthetics of music therapy can be fundamental to the therapeutic process. The consequences of improvising beautiful music may be immeasurable. Discussion and possible affiliations between musicologists and music therapists who improvise should be mutually advantageous. The interactive musical dialogue in improvisation is at the root of creativity in music therapy (Aldridge 1989); it allows individual manifestations of expression – which are at the heart of all musical statements in the clinical process. While the aims and endeavours of music therapists and musicologists may be different, the essential core of their studies is the same. It is this essence that challenges all improvisational approaches to share and learn.

MEANING, PHILOSOPHY AND TONALITY

There are difficulties in trying to appraise music therapy because, of necessity, it becomes affiliated with two potentially opposing disciplines, art and science (Bunt 1994). Music therapy is concerned with human relationships generated through creativity, most therapists formulating an approach that is relevant to their beliefs and the people with whom they work. Differing schools of music therapy serve to provide the bases from which new, ever-evolving approaches may emerge. I believe these approaches should not be seen as exclusively defined. Spitz (1985) suggests that the most valuable way to discover new creative avenues is to retain the theories of one approach while linking them through careful inquiry to another. Bruscia (1989), in his definitions of improvisation in music therapy, attempts to find common and differing themes. His study highlights the positive diversity of music therapy and the insoluble problems faced in attempting to formulate a unified approach. The global survey of music therapy by Moranto (1993) offers definitions of fourteen schools of practice (with sub-categories), which are determined by client populations, psychological theories, treatment goals and clinical approaches. This diversity is also addressed in a recent appraisal by Bunt (1994).

My concern in this chapter is to put forward the musical and personal factors that influence me, and how these affect my work as an improviser in the context of music therapy with the dying. The views presented here are mine alone. I expect some people will find resonance with them and others will disagree; ideas are only of value if they can be challenged and evaluated to influence other ideas.

Music therapy, like art itself, should be ever-changing. Beethoven concisely states: 'Art demands of us that we shall not stand still' (Scott 1934). Methods should be developed only if they can be disseminated to influence and inspire new approaches. Questions can provide answers but also inspire more enlightened questions. Francis was to demand that I re-evaluate the purpose and intent of the music therapy I practised. From how he lived in music – and how it lived in him – he continually challenged me to reconsider the boundaries of our work. He would not rest with any one form of expression and constantly raised the question that my supervisor reiterates to this day: 'Why music?' What are the qualities of music that can so profoundly influence the re-evaluation of the vagaries of life and death and bring healing? The question will remain with me always. It demands constant re-awakenings – to music, to therapy, and to my reactions to the music therapy process itself. The composer Carl Ruggles (Wilson 1964) believed that 'music that does not surge is not great music.' In one sense, that comes close to the depth of my expression as a pianist, composer and music therapist. That surgence of the soul he so intensely captures in his composition 'Sun Treader' is a constant reminder of the emotional force music can transmit. The concentration of this inner disclosing essence is something I constantly strive to achieve: it is the wellspring of my musical life, and source of whatever therapeutic inspiration I can bring to bear.

In a recent publication, I attempted a definition of improvisational music therapy:

> A direct musical link between client and therapist is embodied through the improvisation, the therapist's musical reflections enabling a dynamic interplay to develop within the therapeutic alliance, be it in group or individual work.
>
> (Gilroy and Lee, eds, 1995, p. 3)

Improvisation is the main medium of my work with dying people. It is indispensable to the therapeutic relationship because it affords the client the opportunity of expressing the many facets of living with a terminal diagnosis.

The relationship that comes about through a primarily non-verbal means of communication can be crucial to the expression of issues that are often too difficult or painful to articulate in words.

I have often found myself describing a client's playing as being 'painful'. How do I know, though, that the client is expressing pain? What happens is that I hear and partake in musical expression that causes me to feel pain. This, however, is my interpretation and reaction to the music. So how much is a product of the client's feelings, and how much is projected by the therapist? It is my belief that the interactive processes set up in music-making, and thus the balance between client and therapist, allow the realization of a language that is inherently different from such subjective emotions as pain. Musical language and reflection culminating in the expression of a feeling such as pain become part – but only part – of the overall act of creation. Interpretations are shared between the therapist and client with the intent of refining the necessary balance between explicit and implicit invention. Therapeutically, this idea is controversial, but in philosophical terms it is reflected by Schopenhauer (1819), who stated: 'Music never expresses the phenomenon, but only the inner nature, the in-itself of all phenomena, the will itself.'

This argument leads naturally to discussion of my preoccupation with the musical processes and aesthetics of music therapy. For example, before becoming a music therapist I was always interested in the balance between tonal and atonal music. As a composer, atonality initially influenced my musical growth. But I became concerned that modern music, in the then mid-1970s, did not seem to allow the freedom of ultimately returning to tonality. I remember vividly a composition lesson for which I had carefully prepared a short orchestral piece. My teacher carefully surveyed the score, and his opening comment was that he felt there was an evident lack of black notes! This, he explained, implied tonality, the ensuing silence leaving me in no doubt as to his views on the subject. His criticism typifies the self-imposed musical boundaries that were prevalent at that time. Because of my aversion to such musical straight-jacket ideologies, I not only immersed my musical energies in such composers as Stockhausen, Berio and Boulez, but also in the less strident and more tonally based English tradition of Britten, Maw and Tippett. Through my compositions I searched for atonal avenues while preserving the sense of tonality necessary for creating music that was a true mirror of my music thought. Later as a music therapist I realized the importance of searching between the two polarities. By acknowledging atonality as a part of tonality (Samson 1977) I found a balance that could serve all aspects of music therapy improvisation.

I have chosen an example from a music therapy improvisation (see Figure 2, piano four-hands), to highlight this balance between tonality and atonality. The extract, from my unpublished PhD thesis (Lee 1992), is taken from a session with a client named Eddie. Eddie (player one) improvised atonally while I, the therapist, provided more tonally centred broken chords

Figure 2   Tonality and atonality in improvisation

Fig 2 - 3 -

culminating in a hymn-like figure at 7:50. The general tonality of the passage is D flat. The difference of musical content between client and therapist provided a powerful therapeutic effect that formed the basis, within the research, of an in-depth analysis.

The large majority of music therapy improvisation is tonally based. Paul Nordoff's teachings on musical resources (Nordoff and Robbins 1977) developed from a long history based on the romantic tradition, leaving modern classical music mostly untouched. His work heightened my urge to look more closely at atonally influenced music. I tackled this by applying the techniques of acquiring musical resources suggested by Nordoff and Robbins (1977) to present-day composers. In adapting this approach to the music of such composers as Boulez and Birtwistle, and through practice and experience in sessions, my feeling for a balance between tonality and atonality began to develop. The more confident I became, the easier it was to include these musical influences spontaneously within sessions. I never tried to enforce the style; it became instead a resource that could be drawn on when appropriate. Subsequently, my improvisational skills began to mature into a way of working that could accommodate the clinical situation while remaining true to myself as a musician and composer. This combining of traditional and contemporary resources consolidated further in my work at London Lighthouse. As I worked with people with HIV and AIDS, particularly musicians such as Francis, the approach became finely tuned.

Through the analyses of my research (Lee 1992) I began to examine the complexities of musical components in improvisation. Witold Lutoslawski poses a question specifically related to pitch and harmony:

> In my opinion the traditional scale with its twelve notes has not yet been fully exploited in terms of harmony. I believe that there are still many possibilities to be discovered, independently from the Schoenberg twelve-tone technique.
>
> (Lutoslawski 1988, composer's note).

I am convinced that music therapists should constantly be questioning and re-evaluating their musical understanding. If an improvisation is in a particular idiom or mode, the musical and/or therapeutic enigma should not only be considered in broad terms, but also in regard to the expressive details, the smallest musical components. Observing how such components affect the therapeutic process cannot but give music therapists greater insight into their work. Detailed musical inquiry must invite more refined listening. One way in which a music therapist might approach this is to assess where an improvisation lies along a continuum that moves from a style that is clearly tonal, through atonality with strong tonal inferences, to a tonal centre with atonal connections. There are infinitesimal gradients along this scale, all of which can be treated openly with an equal emphasis of questioning.

MUSIC THERAPY IN PALLIATIVE CARE – IMPROVISATION

The growth of music therapy in palliative/hospice care has been rich and diverse (Bailey 1983, 1984, 1985, Bright 1986, Fagen 1982, Forinash 1990, Frank 1985, Gilbert 1977, Kerkvliet 1972, Magill-Levreault 1993, Mandel 1991, Munro 1978, 1984, 1988, 1994, O'Callaghan 1984, 1989, 1990, 1993, Whittal 1990). The main concentrations of music therapists have developed in Australia, Canada and the USA. In the UK, over the past three years, there has been a growing interest in the potential of using music therapy in hospices, and there are several therapists currently employed in this field. Documented work was spearheaded by Munro (1978). Her initial predictions for the possible uses of music in a therapeutic setting fall into four main areas: physical, psychological, social and spiritual. The therapeutic guidelines adopted to serve these categories were developed mainly from the use of pre-recorded and pre-composed music.

In 1989, the first symposium for music therapists working in palliative care was held at the Calvary Hospital, New York (Martin, ed., 1989). During the symposium people met to collate and compare differing methods and techniques of practice. What ensued was a list of therapeutic approaches that ranged from the use of simple improvisational techniques, pre-composed and pre-recorded music, through to using the sounds of natural environments, and the combination of music and massage. Clarification of definitions of practice, when the term 'music therapy' is used to cover such a range of approaches, is fraught with complication. O'Callaghan (1989) notes that while the initial writings on music therapy and the dying have provided a solid grounding of documentation and description, a serviceable music therapy framework has still to be formulated. A group of recent articles (Magill-Levreault 1993, Mandel 1993, O'Callaghan 1993, Salmon 1993) have begun to shed more light on the intricacies of using music therapy with the dying. Munro's documentation in the *Oxford Textbook of Palliative Medicine* (1994) provides a concise survey of all aspects of musical and non-musical intervention with suggested possibilities for research. In 1994 an international conference on music therapy in palliative care was held in Oxford. The diversity of papers further highlighted the enormous potential for expansion in therapeutic practice and research (Lee, ed., 1995).

Improvisation as a therapeutic medium has rarely been mentioned in the literature. In 1984 Munro stated: 'Improvisation, which I had hoped to use often, was only very infrequently an appropriate therapeutic technique with these very ill patients. I certainly needed to adjust my expectations in this regard' (Munro 1984, p. 84). This statement encapsulates the then generally held belief that for people who were this ill, improvisation was not an appropriate therapeutic approach. In a later publication, however, Munro reconsiders in greater depth the dynamics of improvisation:

Instrumental improvisation, here defined as the unpracticed, spontaneous playing of instruments, offers an avenue for expression and communication and encourages mobility and motivation. The availability of a variety of good-quality instruments, which do not necessarily require previous musical or instrumental skills, is essential. In this kind of improvisation, sound 'pictures' are spontaneously searched for and created. Their content may express non-verbally what cannot easily be put into words, or may repeat and reinforce what has been said before in other ways. Such improvisation allows the possibility of experiencing and accepting 'imperfect' music, just as emotions and thoughts are often 'imperfect', compared to perceived standards. This method holds a potent key to unconscious issues which are not easily addressed verbally, namely anger, jealousy, existential loneliness, and fear.

(Munro 1994, p. 556)

Salmon (1993) also emphasizes the potential of improvisation by citing a case study of music therapy with a lonely young man with a malignant melanoma. Steven played guitar and piano. Salmon describes an improvisation with Steven at the piano and herself playing the flute:

Steven took the lead, beginning with a safe, predictable C major chord progression. I followed, melodically, on my flute. As the music unfolded, it became more and more atonal, arrhythmic, fast and loud. At one point, Steven was practically pounding on the piano. I supported and reflected what I felt as tremendous rage, inserting disjointed, high and fast passages on the flute. After a few minutes of this, Steven abruptly changed the music, returning to a chorale-like harmonization in C major. We ended quietly and peacefully.

(Salmon 1993, p. 49)

HIV AND AIDS

My first experience of using improvisation with a client living with AIDS, and who was close to death, was distressing and difficult. John was referred to me as having no musical expertise but much anger and frustration. Although he was staying on the residential unit at London Lighthouse and was very ill, he insisted that he have a session in the music therapy room rather than the ward, even though the physical effort to get there required much courage. He seemed to be in constant pain.

To my surprise his playing was immediate, loud and scattered. He used unpitched percussion while I attempted to match his dynamics on the piano. His playing was clearly directed toward me, the therapist. For our immediate musical relationship he used me as a target to focus his loud aggressive phrases. While I recognized the need he had to direct his feelings toward one person, rather than express himself in vague broader terms, I was shocked to find how much this process drained me. In contrast to his outburst of dynamic musical searching, he later expressed himself through two beautifully controlled, quiet, introvert piano solos.

We shared two more sessions, John dying three days after our third. He neither spoke nor requested interpretation of the music during our time together. The sessions I shared with him set the future direction of my work. He showed me that improvisation could provide a means of exploring unresolved issues even when a person is ill and near death. The dawning that came after his death was that my personality as a music therapist and my personal life as an individual could not be lived separately. I had to allow my uncertainties, professionally and personally, to affect and influence my response.

I find it important to stress that my experiences confirm that verbal explorations in music therapy are secondary to musical explorations. In my work, improvisation is not considered as a channel toward words, but as the source of its own unique experiences and processes. However, verbal interpretations are not excluded, and if a client wishes to discuss a musical experience I will accommodate this need. Should this happen, I will not offer assessments or interpretations of the musical material accessible on the sessional recordings. If either client or therapist feels that more in-depth verbal evaluation is needed, the client may be referred to a verbal therapist. The experience of working with John gave me a therapeutic direction rooted in musical experience. There are times when a client's self-expression culminates in rich complexities of music-making, yet there are other times when self-expression moves toward silence. Whichever path is taken and whatever objectives are decided upon, the source remains the same, that of a creative musical relationship.

The following verbal explorations, offered spontaneously by three clients, further confirm the versatility and effectiveness of an improvisational approach:

> Through music therapy I am learning to express myself in a way that I didn't know existed. Expressing a part of me I never thought I had. My music has become a very important part of me. When I was diagnosed as having the HIV infection two years ago, I knew I had to do something about it. Music therapy has been a fulfilling, exciting and truly wonderful addition to my life. It's added a new dimension and has proved therapeutically to be an excellent means of alleviating stress.

> I have been on a long journey during the past eight years and now it is my chosen task to find a form of creative expression in which I may find the inside of me. Music therapy for me is about a common language of understanding that will lead to the heart, leaving the intellect free to do only the work it was designed to do, as a servant of the heart. Music therapy allows me the access to a self-remembering of the past data held in my mind. It is this data that has a form and symmetry to it. A

path of random symmetry that means for just a very brief moment you can almost see the essence coming from me.

The anger that I feel, which is portrayed musically in a mainly disjointed fashion, is to do with my own fears of my illness and the possible repercussions for me. I can express my fears through improvising without having to verbally spell them out.

Underlying the transformation of ideas and experiences that have taken place over the years, the following principles have proven to be constant:

– that music therapy provides a space for growth when potentially all around is shrinking.
– that music therapy works not only with issues of death and dying but with health and life.
– that music therapy can facilitate an in-depth relationship between therapist and client built non-verbally. During the dying process this relationship can generate an intensity of understanding that is profound and unique.
– that music therapy asks no questions and makes no demands, it simply enables the person to be. For people living with a terminal illness this can be important.

Tippett, in his collection of essays entitled *Music of the Angels* (1980), evaluates the experience of art:

To a certain degree all appreciation of art is escapism – to leave behind the world of matter-of-fact. The important question is always: escape into what? Escape into the true inner world of feelings is one of the most rewarding experiences known to man. When entry into this world is prevented, and still more when it is unsought, a man is certainly to some degree unfulfilled.

(Tippett 1980, p. 21)

When working with dying people I am always acutely aware of trying to offer that experience of escaping from the world of external reality into the more intangible breadth of music. It is my belief that the inner world of music has no element of illness and so at its most essential level offers a release that is both liberating and spiritual. I recently had the privilege of working with a young girl who was dying from a large tumour. The physical manifestations of her illness were so acute that they dominated her inner as well as her outer life. Through improvisation she was able to loosen the shackles of her painful daily existence and enter into realms of musical expression that she described, like many before her, as being 'like flying'. It is the metaphor of flying that so accurately symbolizes the flow of music immediately available through improvisation.

In my improvisational practice, weekly sessions are held at the same time, in the same room, and last one hour. Clients do not need to be musical, though any knowledge and expertise is accommodated within the therapeutic process. A variety of instruments is available to both client and therapist: the piano, pitched and unpitched percussion, simple wind instruments and the voice. The instruments are chosen specifically to enable the client to enter into musical expression without previous knowledge or training. Each session, and improvisation within a session, is a self-contained experience with its own validity; it springs from and contributes to the therapeutic process as a whole. The therapist will normally wait until the client begins to improvise, then his or her role becomes active in supporting and responding to the client's musical expression.

With the client's permission, sessions are recorded. The purpose is twofold: firstly for the client to access recordings for self-evaluation, and secondly for the therapist's professional assessment. The practice of improvisational music therapy requires the therapist to listen back to sessions in order to monitor the ongoing therapeutic process. The recordings hold up a mirror to the sessional work; they provide a means of precise clinical perception that counterbalances the freedom of the creative process. Recording-based documentation and evaluation enable the therapist to consider in greater depth the complexities of the client's musical engagement. Without this continued evaluation it is impossible to perceive or maintain the therapy process as an organic development from session to session. Similarly, a client may wish to listen back to the music in between sessions in order to re-live and re-examine important experiences. High-quality recording equipment should be used. Recordings also provide, again with the client's permission, researchers, students, instructors, allied professionals, and the general public with opportunities to experience the power of the therapeutic interaction in a way not otherwise possible. Occasionally, for personal reasons a client may ask that a session not be recorded, a wish that the therapist must honour.

CONCLUDING COMMENTS

The differing practices in Europe and America in working with people with HIV and AIDS have demonstrated the validity of two distinctly different music therapy approaches. Music therapists in America have developed their practice in the main through Guided Imagery and Music (GIM), which is essentially based on selective listening and musically facilitated in-depth counselling (Bruscia 1991, 1995b),[1] whereas music therapists in Europe have found creative intervention based on improvisation to be their most effective form of therapeutic procedure (Aldridge and Neugebauer 1990, Lee 1989, 1990, 1991, 1992).

HIV and AIDS have strong social and stigmatizing implications that can adversely affect the therapeutic process. The music therapist may experience what has been termed the 'AIDS dream' (Winarski 1991) and sleepless nights.

Overwhelming feelings of helplessness brought on by the recognition that a client will eventually die can produce distress that will restrict the therapeutic relationship. Physical deterioration, possible dementia, and the unwillingness of the therapist to face these manifestations as heralding the end of the therapeutic relationship, can bring complex personal issues to the fore. As death approaches, it can become practically difficult to continue the regularity of sessions; the client may be hospitalized or too ill to attend. The therapist then experiences new anxieties. Uncertainty as to whether the client will be able to attend sessions, and the possibility that he or she may have died become frighteningly real. At this time the client may become distanced, provoking fears of rejection. Saying goodbye can also have lasting repercussions for the music therapist. How is the subject broached? What words are adequate to express the end of a relationship that has been built primarily through music? Often words are not exchanged, leaving the therapist with open questions that will need to be addressed in supervision or counselling.

In all aspects of palliative care, music therapy requires a defined and carefully monitored therapeutic practice. The qualities of music can act as a bridge between the natural forces of life and the spiritual dimensions of dying. How does the music therapist move between the man-made world of music and everyday life, through to the silence captured in death? Francis's story is about two people who, through music, touched this membrane. It is my hope that through experiencing this intense therapeutic journey, the reader will gain insight into the process of music therapy with the dying. I have tried within this chapter, and throughout the book as a whole, to allow my thoughts and experiences to emerge in a way that is true both to Francis and to myself as a music therapist and an individual.

3

CREATIVITY AND CHAOS – ASSESSMENT AND SESSIONS ONE TO FIVE

The divine inspiration of music, poetry, and painting do not arrive at perfection by degrees, like the other sciences, but by starts, and like flashes of lightning, one here, another there, appear in various lands, then suddenly vanish.

Pierre de Ronsard (1524–1560)
Dedication to 'Livre des Melanges', 1560

MEETING

My first encounter with Francis took place on the day of an official visit to London Lighthouse by the Princess of Wales. I had returned from my holidays the previous week to be met with an urgent message on my answer machine saying that a sudden royal visit had been planned for the following Thursday. The timetable was to include a visit to music therapy, the Princess having shown an interest in meeting myself and some clients. The morning itself was frenetic; the room had to be completely re-arranged and the two clients who had agreed to meet the Princess of Wales became extremely nervous. The atmosphere was fraught with tension, though the event itself took place simply and quickly. The emotional intensity, however, left me exhausted and drained.

I was attempting to re-create normality when a man strode into the music therapy room. He immediately informed me that his name was Francis. His opening gambit was confrontational, a monologue that permitted no response from me. His tone was unemotional, each word spoken with a quiet deliberation. He explained that he had AIDS and that he was staying for a two-week respite period on the residential unit. He held himself in a way that belied his frailty and emphasized a presence that was immediately imposing. He seemed conscious of his appearance and spoke with a measured assurance that completely confounded my previous experiences of a person with AIDS. First, he was middle-aged, and second, his intellectual capacity from the first words he uttered felt superior to my own. He went on to say that he had heard that music therapy was available and since I had not visited the unit that

28

morning to see if he would like to attend, he had decided that he would find me. The impatience in his voice made me realize that it was no good using the Princess of Wales as an excuse: I had not been accessible when he needed me. Francis went on to demand a clear and concise definition of music therapy. He wanted to know how it could be of help to him. To have to explain music therapy in not more than two sentences, as is so often a music therapist's brief, is difficult at the best of times. To satisfy this assertive client, I knew that my answer would have to be extraordinarily precise and articulate, in spite of my exhaustion. Steadying myself, I explained simply that music therapy at Lighthouse was available to allow people to explore their feelings mainly through improvisation. Furthermore, that while words were not excluded, the potential power of music therapy lay in the fact that one could express emotions without words. During my brief explanation I endured a stare of frightening intensity.

The next sentence Francis spoke had an enormous impact on me. He revealed that he had studied piano to a professional standard, his whole demeanour suggesting that he was anticipating an impressed response. For the first time in my professional life I wanted to run, escape and get away. How could I work with such grandiosity and aggression? A feeling welled up that made me determined I was *not* going to improvise with this man if his musical abilities were as good as he intimated. I felt threatened and vulnerable. My dread resulted in a few inarticulate remarks. To my surprise he requested a session later that day. I don't remember organizing it other than we finished by deciding that three o'clock would be the most appropriate time. Once this had been arranged he left. It looked as though I was fated to improvise with this man after all. My heart sank.

I entered the session with great trepidation, a natural reaction to my ordeal earlier in the day. However, Francis was initially less challenging, as if I had passed some test. He explained that he had studied piano at the Guildhall School of Music and Drama in his late twenties. He stressed the problems he had faced from family and friends in aspiring to be a professional musician. Shortly after completing his studies he became an interpreter – he spoke six languages – and emigrated to Rio de Janeiro. Disillusioned with music, he had not subsequently played the piano for about fifteen years. When he discovered he was HIV positive he decided to return to England and had now been back just over two years. Listening, I realized that he had enormous apprehensions about re-establishing a connection with music. Why had he made contact with me? What was he hoping to gain by rekindling an area of his life that had been so obviously difficult? We remained silent, neither of us being able to provide a satisfactory answer to this opening enigma.

He went on to tell me that he had recently received a diagnosis of AIDS and proceeded to explain what this disturbing information would mean for his future. It is unusual for a client to speak so clearly about death and dying within a first meeting. His dispassionate commentary on the fact that he was dying was the beginning of his testing of my professional role. He asked if it upset me to hear him discuss death and dying, further inquiring as to my own HIV status. He said he was not sure that I could fully understand his predicament unless I too was living with HIV or AIDS. This direct challenge was not uncommon though never before had a client instigated the issue so directly and so soon.

His question raised perhaps the most fundamental aspect of working with other people's problems. How can anyone fully understand another person's perceptions unless they too have had the same experiences? Of course the answer is one can't. All one can do is to be there as fully and deeply as possible. My instinct was to say that of course I had speculated many times about what it would be like to be HIV positive and how that might have affected my work, but I decided to be totally honest. I explained that to the best of my knowledge I didn't have the virus and hoped that he wouldn't regard this as being unsympathetic. I ventured to say that my skills as a music therapist would be available if we worked together, but that I couldn't accommodate his projections of my supposed lack of complete sympathy with his situation. The silence that ensued was the first of many such challenging spaces. His eyes darted about the room as he struggled for a response. He looked angry and confused. My reaction had come from a primitive sense of survival that I immediately regretted. To my surprise he calmly agreed with my interpretation, saying that he had only been interested in how I would react to such a difficult scenario. The conversation continued to feel like some kind of inquisition and I began to feel indignant.

Without giving me a chance to respond, Francis changed the direction of our discussion by asking me to expound in greater detail on music therapy, specifically improvisation. Drawing breath and calming myself, I explained that improvisation was important as it provided an experience that was both ongoing and of the moment, and it was possible to realize the actual moment of expression on many different levels. Through improvisation one could demonstrate and feel a whole range of emotions either singly or collectively. It was these simple yet complex limits, I explained, that kept the essential immediacy that was so crucial in the work I was doing at Lighthouse. He said he understood but felt unable to comment until he had directly experienced improvisation for himself.

With a sense of foreboding I told him that I had not worked with a musician before. Through his stare I realized that this did not please him. In an effort to retrieve some credibility I explained that as a part of my work at Lighthouse I was evaluating the effectiveness of music therapy for a doctoral research project. This, to some extent, seemed to appease him. He said that he felt unable to improvise; he had been taught that improvisation was a specialist area for jazz musicians or those exceptionally talented within specific stylistic confines. Even though my earlier feeling had been that improvising with him would be a severe test of my own skills, I heard myself suggesting that we might take time within this assessment session to improvise together. He reluctantly agreed and after a short deliberation we decided to improvise with Francis on percussion (side-drum, congas, xylophone and gong), and myself on piano.

He was right to be hesitant; his uncertainty during our first exploration was reflected in cumbersome and stilted playing. My musical contribution was equally stagnant. The music remained unfocused and scattered. It is quite normal during a first improvisation for there to be a certain amount of hesitancy, though Francis's playing displayed a tenseness that appeared to be related to the instruments he was using. I struggled to find a musical structure where we might begin to achieve a semblance of unity. The improvisation lasted about ten minutes. At the end he remained silent for a few moments before gently but firmly saying 'No.' By now the trepidation with which I had begun the session was so intense that his response did not seem to matter. The situation felt irretrievable and I was convinced that at any moment he would leave. This day had been a whirlwind: first the Princess of Wales and now this extraordinary testing. All I wanted was some peace and space. I said nothing as there was nothing to say.

To my surprise he requested that, if we had time, he would like to try another improvisation. My impulse was to refuse, as I felt it would be a lot easier if he just left and never returned. As it was, however, I agreed. He looked directly at me as if waiting for a firm lead, but when I did not intervene he took the initiative and asked that we improvise together at the piano. This was more hopeful as I knew from experience that the combination of therapist and client together at one keyboard can be fruitful. There is something about the physical closeness and sharing of one musical territory that can bring about far-reaching results. I desperately hoped this would be the case, only in this instance I felt a lack of parity. Francis instructed me to play the bass of the piano while he played the treble.

From the moment we started the second improvisation, a stream of musical expression poured from him. Our relationship took on a completely new dimension, one of union and solidarity. The structure of the music instantly merged, as if it had always had been there and we had simply reached out and caught it. My own musical awareness soon became a part of the whole, instinctively letting go of the constraints I felt he had placed upon me through words. The music soared, taking on its own organic direction that neither of us was able to affect. Feelings of severity and joy, anguish and exhilaration raced through my head. Here was a musical oneness I had never experienced on such a level before. The improvisation lasted approximately twenty minutes, leaving us both exhausted but revitalized.

The silence after the improvisation seemed to last as long as the music itself. Francis bowed his head as I caught my breath in anticipation of his response. Silences were to become a prominent and essential part of our work. They were some of the most difficult times for me as therapist, and

31

seemed to encapsulate the essence of the preceding music itself. He seemed to relish an almost theatrical quiet before he calmly said, 'I would like another session. If that is possible, what would be the best time for you next week?' I consulted my diary. 'Twelve o'clock would be good,' I replied. With that he steadily rose to his feet and left the room. Sitting glued to the piano stool I could do nothing but watch this frail man slowly make his way to the door. The adage that appearances are deceiving had never seemed so appropriate. I felt as if I had been left in mid-air, a feeling that was to continue throughout the day. This had been one of my most arduous but inspirational days as a music therapist and was to be the beginning of one of the most challenging experiences of my life.

SESSION ONE – FIRST STEP

Within my day's work at Lighthouse, a ten-minute break was scheduled between sessions. This time gave me the opportunity to make any necessary re-arrangements to the musical instruments, and check the recording equipment, as well as providing a space for personal stillness before the next client. The morning I was next due to see Francis was difficult. It had been hard to focus on the two sessions before and I was aware of reservations in my response to clients' needs. My thoughts kept returning to what might lie ahead in Francis's first session and the overriding feeling that I was about to embark on a journey that would demand every facet of my skills as a music therapist. I knew instinctively that my musicianship would be stretched to its limit and had doubts as to whether I would be able to match and reflect his precise use of words. My recollection of the preliminary session was that it had been difficult and searching. The dynamic second improvisation had retrieved what could have been a disastrous meeting. Despite the musical unity we had achieved, I half hoped that he wouldn't arrive. I felt apprehensive.

Leaving the music therapy room, I noticed him sitting alone in the reception area. An overriding sense of anxiety made me consider retreating before he saw me. Recognizing the irrationality of these thoughts I steadied myself and approached him. Our conversation was brief; we exchanged greetings and acknowledged that the session would begin in ten minutes. He requested that we meet outside the music therapy room at the allotted time. Returning, I nervously watched the minutes tick by until midday and the beginning of the session.

As he entered, Francis immediately began to discuss the second improvisation of the assessment session. He explained that the music had directly influenced him during the week. After much thought he had decided that, if it was possible, he would like to continue exploring through music, a medium that he felt, until now, he had lost. I was surprised that he had such a positive approach even though my own recollection was that the piano improvisation had indeed been compelling. We therefore agreed that the sessions would be ongoing and that from now on all the work would be recorded.

He went on to explain that during our discussion in the assessment session he had consciously pushed me away:

> 'I was feeling unwell last week. One has different ways of feeling unwell. In this instance I couldn't communicate with people. To listen to someone else was too much. There were moments when I let you in and moments when there wasn't room. For me that's all right, the feelings of "how dare you do that" in therapy don't apply. I wanted you to feel that kind of rejection. I was in some ways testing you.'

I was relieved to hear his admission:

> 'Were you aware that you were blocking me out?'

> 'Yes I was. I wasn't blocking you out I was blocking myself in, a subtle difference I think. I wasn't saying "I won't let this son of a bitch in," I was trying to set rules for you, perhaps for us both. I wasn't consciously listening or considering you. The good thing was that you weren't intrusive. You were low key.'

This conversation set the limits for our first stage of work. My thoughts focused on the possibility that his testing was an indication of his need to feel secure within the sessions. Verbally, the first ten sessions were to be difficult. Before my involvement with Francis I had worked with great resolve at the musical components of improvisation, believing that music therapy could be embraced within essentially musical parameters. I was confident of my ability to improvise to a high musical standard and had not promoted verbal dialogue more than a client desired. Now being tested similarly in words I felt that failing this test could weaken or even invalidate the relationship. Through my counselling I had begun to explore my hesitation in using words. Would it be necessary to re-evaluate my own particular philosophy about music therapy? I.e., that its framework cannot be compared with verbal therapies and that improvisation works within an infrastructure that is unique to itself. While my assumption was that improvisation would be the focal point of our work, I began to realize that spoken reflections would demand equal skills. The search for a balance between words and music continued and intensified during these initial sessions.

Francis described how the first improvisation in the assessment session, in which while I had played piano he had played percussion, had left him feeling unsatisfied:

> 'The percussion for me was far less responsive than the piano. I felt inhibited in trying to express myself. It is my feeling that these instruments will block any musical or therapeutic direction I might want to

33

make. If there is no obligation to include the percussion I would like to propose that I use only the piano.'

His request was not unexpected. The duet with percussion had been awkward in comparison with the piano-duet, which was instantly expressive and transparent. My view was that Francis was correct in his assumptions. I agreed to his proposal, deciding that any problems arising from it would have to be addressed later.

Before the first improvisation he discussed the idea of confining the music to a predetermined scale:

> 'I think it might be a good idea if we restrict the tones we use. The piano improvisation last week was completely free. I would like to balance that experience with something that is more limited, in a sense that I can balance that perception with an expression that is more contained . . . The scale that immediately comes to mind is the whole-tone scale . . . What do you think?'[1]

I was surprised:

> 'I think the whole-tone scale is very powerful.'
> 'Yes I agree . . . My only problem with restricting is that I will immediately want to do something different. Anyway let's try.'

Throughout the improvisation, in which Francis played treble and I the bass, we held our own musical identities. Through my playing I encouraged him to improvise in an opposing manner to me, while I sought to offer the experience of both partnership and independence. My music was acquiescent and static, in contrast to his, which was powerfully rhythmic and resolute. The few times we united were balanced against long periods of contrast. I intentionally did not intrude upon his area of musical expression or limit his independence in the musical relationship.

This opposition in musical communication, that I have elsewhere termed 'antithetical expression' (Lee 1992b), was a factor that was to become crucial to my work, not only in my relationship with Francis, but with all my clients with HIV and AIDS. The idea of opposing aspects of life (Jung 1963, 1972) can be directly related to improvisation in music therapy: 'The therapist must be concerned with but at the same time impartial to the client' (Cox 1978). Clients discussed the often contradictory aspects of musical communication from different viewpoints. Francis talked in terms of 'darkness and light', while others described it in terms of 'aggression and calm' or 'as a journey from one state to another'. I wondered if the connection between musical and therapeutic opposites might have a direct relation to the representation of illness and death and dying. As my therapy practice and research progressed I found that many clients battled with two sides of their persona when coming to terms with living with HIV and AIDS. This was often manifested through the musical relationship at both a simple and a profound level.

After the improvisation Francis described his feelings about the opposing expression:

'I was thinking of our playing in terms of darkness and light. I thought that the music disclosed two sides of my musical and therapeutic expression. I saw them as being separate, yet integrated . . . I suppose it could be possible to see one or either – playing together or playing apart – as positive or negative. I would however not consider opposites in these terms, rather as differing polarities of communication. It appeared that this contradictory expression formed the crux of the improvisation.'

As we continued exploring the consequences of improvising within the whole-tone scale, he commented:

'The whole-tone scale has a very special sound . . . Perhaps too special. I found it rather difficult to express my true feelings through this enforced containment. I found it a bit of a strait-jacket to live in, though perhaps it could possibly help you to balance something else. I found that there wasn't much room for diversification. The music was very much in the same mood.'
'Would you have liked it to change?'
'At first yes, but then I realized that there wasn't room somehow. I became limited in a sense that I couldn't find a way to break out because the whole-tone scale is so distinctive in the way that the tones are arranged. I found myself accommodating my emotions within the limits of the music – even though for the most part I wanted to express something else. It did hinder me, but conversely it gave me the experience I wanted: the difference between freedom and constriction. That in itself has been a useful exercise though one, I suspect, that I will not often want to repeat.'

Improvising within the bounds of a limited scale, mode or harmonic sequence can be therapeutically positive or negative. As an improvisational approach it can be confining if not handled with care. If the needs of the client dictate musical limits then the therapist should be aware that certain musical formulae, such as whole-tone or pentatonic scales, can often be difficult to withdraw from.

In the second improvisation I played treble, Francis bass; he had the sustaining pedal. There were no set musical limits; antithetical expression again formed the basic structure of the piece.

1 **Audio Extract One – Session One (6:39)**
(Three minutes after the opening)

- Tonal centres moving between E minor and C major.
- Both players are thematically independent. Legato themes (bass) alongside the development of a rhythmic melody (treble):

There is a sense of moving forward.
- The music builds to a climax after which the intensity subsides toward a short pause.
- The phrases are detached, the treble developing a syncopated rhythmic figure:

- The bass enforces a ritardando. There is a diminuendo. After an increase in tempo the rhythm becomes regular.
- The music as a whole becomes more unified. The improvisation is urgent and energetic.
- The music fades quickly toward an extended silence.
- The next section begins quietly. The bass provides warm romantic phrases over which the treble improvises long melodic lines.
- The music becomes impassioned with a march-like figure in the middle register.
- An extended tremolo (treble), provides the bass with the opportunity to improvise long arched phrases. The tremolo figure then moves to the bass.
- The music becomes quieter before building toward a climax.
- There is a recapitulation of the melodic and tremolo accompaniment.
     (The improvisation continues for ten minutes after the extract.)

Francis was enthralled:

'It's amazing how quickly we musically came together . . . I wasn't aware of a key. I think that if you are aware of the possibilities of keys you can then throw them away. In improvisation there are needs to re-work and revise the idea of formalized scales. There can be a dominating tone structure from which you can then be free. Of course the structure can still be there, but you wander in and out freely without being tied to any specific rule. It felt in a key, but I don't think it was. It was related somehow. It was interesting that our roles again were musically differ-

36

ent, there was a sense of togetherness that came from independence. It would be wrong to say at this stage that I am directly expressing my fears of loss and endings. I am trying to create quality music and that is all ... Perhaps subconsciously the music is a product of my psychological state, I'm not sure ... I have a feeling that I will be able to assess the moulding of music and therapy as the relationship develops. For now I am happy to think and respond in purely musical terms.

He left in high spirits while I felt as if all my energy had been expended. Walking the streets of Notting Hill later, I reflected on the immensity of the journey ahead.

SESSION TWO – FINDING A VOICE

I found it difficult to shed my emotional responses when working with people with HIV and AIDS; the music remained with me on various levels during the week. The intensity of the meeting often left me with introspective questions, and oftentimes the need for isolation and quiet. I do not think I was seeking resolution, it was rather that the particular quality of togetherness so often experienced in and through music sharing, left a deep impression that needed processing during the week. The counselling I received was essential for these explorations. The emotions were at times uncomfortable, but they were necessary in evaluating the issues facing me as a music therapist. It is essential for therapists to explore why they have chosen to work with a particular client group and indeed why they initially decided to become a therapist. My own reasons were based around fears of death and dying. To work with people whose main concerns are endings requires an ability to face the inevitability of death and dying. This is disturbing and can seem to be insurmountable, a sentiment that does not diminish with time or experience.

During the week following the first session I experienced mixed emotions. On one level it was satisfying that I had been able to provide Francis with the opportunity to begin his musical journey. On another I was daunted by the suspicion that this was probably just the beginning of his testing. Overall, however, we had clearly begun to establish a structure, the improvisations already providing periods of mutual musical excitement.

Early in the second session, Francis began with another request to confine the musical bounds of an improvisation:

'Last week we worked within the whole-tone scale which I found rather unsatisfactory. I am still interested however in exploring the ideas of working within an imposed structure. I thought that we might try an improvisation that was simply based around a single tone so that the base of the music will be pivoted around it, a sort of colossal tonic. It is an idea that I have been considering during the week and would like to

37

examine its potential before I possibly dismiss it . . . I think it is always a good idea to go with your initial instincts, and my first thought is E flat.'

The improvisation with Francis in the treble, myself in the bass, began with a small rhythmic motive initiated by him, based melodically and harmonically on the imposed tonic, E flat. This provided the material for the first section, the music later becoming freer and less concerned with the dictates of the rhythmic opening. The E flat core was eventually abandoned, the improvisation drawing inconclusively to a close. Francis was thoughtful:

'That was sparse, rather like Stravinsky. I felt it had a critical open texture and there was an interesting combination of tones based mainly on the major second. The rhythmic elements were reminiscent to me of a cake-walk. I didn't get carried away – but that often happens when you are expressing an emotion. You don't actually want to touch it. You don't want to be overwhelmed by it because it sparks off an almost stand-off feeling. You can feel the anger or disruption through displaced recognition.'
'Recognition, but not touching?'
'Yes, once removed. Not allowing yourself to take an overtly romantic descent . . . I didn't feel inclined to move into hymnals or overt expressions. I think there was quite a sharing of ideas, that unlike last week was more united.'

The idea of not representing an emotion directly through music was a view Francis became extremely concerned with. He felt that expressing a feeling somehow betrayed the intensity of the emotion itself, that the strength of expression through music was more complex than just depiction. The power of his improvisations lay in the fact that he often translated into music views that were in opposition to the nature of the expression itself. This realization opened up new avenues for me concerning therapeutic meaning and musical description. I began to realize the dynamics of improvisation in music therapy were more complex and diverse than I had previously thought. It was this powerful learning from the client that was to prove such a important force in our work together.

The second improvisation had no limits. The first part was meditative, leading toward a passage that was assertive and less tonally centred. The opening reflective music acted as an anchor to which the improvisation continually returned. After its conclusion Francis's analysis was penetrating:

'When I'm improvising and think of a musical idea that is not appropriate, I sometimes think in a split-second, "No, I mustn't do that!" Then I realize that it is pointless to visualize in these terms. Why should I repress my musical feelings? If it occurs, it occurs . . . We were in a less Wagnerian mood than last week. The music felt more neoclassical, quite different in mood. It had a clear texture because you could easily hear what was going on. It's as if we are being more open about our relationship, perhaps more ready to accept each other now.'

I remember at this time considering the significance of his use of composers' idiosyncratic styles in formulating his perceptions. Describing the musical events of music therapy in terms of composers and styles was something that had not occurred before. While this could be viewed as a distraction from the therapeutic process, I instinctively knew that it was a valuable development. There was inspiration and clarity in relating the thematic ideas of improvisation to past periods and forms.

The third improvisation, in which Francis took the treble and I the bass, began with him discovering a theme of fast-moving arpeggios. The texture became dense, leading to a section that was without meter or tonal centre. This was reminiscent of the four-hand improvisation in session one. The concluding passage reiterated the opening theme, the arpeggios now improvised in the bass over which Francis wove a simple melody in octaves. After the improvisation he was enthusiastic:

> 'This improvisation felt more like an accurate transcription of my feelings. There is a kind of difficulty in the acceptance acquired through strength from withdrawal. The positive aspects of saying "no", a very positive "no". At the same time I'm feeling that I'm giving up on some things and giving up on some battles. That I can build on that too and be more myself. That is the paradox of living. It's an extraordinary thing to express these feelings on the piano . . . We played well together in this session. I feel that it was very thought-provoking . . . I am aware that we didn't do much talking in this session, there didn't seem the need.'

Searching my feelings after the session and during my counselling, I began to consider that perhaps Francis was exploring his own musical and emotional limitations, evaluating how each influenced the other within the framework of words and music. It sometimes felt as if he was avoiding the possibility for real musical communication, that he would reach out but then withdraw from the thing he most wanted to touch, musical union. While I would never have raised this issue within the session it was important for me to think about and view our work from as many different angles as possible. I subsequently challenged my assumption. Perhaps Francis was finding his own level within the therapeutic relationship? Whichever way I turned and viewed the widening sphere of our work, this session did feel more focused: a stage removed from the control he had exerted on the music in the first session.

SESSION THREE – CHALLENGES AND SOLOS

My anxiety lessened before this session. Counselling had assisted me in exploring how our work might find its balance. It became clear that I had been

trying to apply my present understanding of music therapy, instead of allowing the process to find its own level. Staying with the evolving musical expression, however difficult, became essential. Allowing the next cycle to move
naturally was one of the most powerful lessons at this stage in our work. This
realization allowed me to relax and trust the moment. My new-found
awareness, however, was soon to be tested. Francis entered the session
nervously and obviously needed to talk:

> 'My week has been very stressful. I decided after our last session that
> I wanted my own piano again. It's been fifteen years since I've played
> and considerably longer than that since I've had my own instrument.
> I have some savings you see, and so I thought, "I have never given
> myself anything and it will be a very good going away present" . . . [he
> laughed]. The only problem was that I chose a piano from the show-
> rooms and it was delivered immediately. It all happened so fast, that
> before I knew what had happened it was on my doorstep. I had to
> buy an upright because it has to be housed in my bedroom. I have a
> room in a vicarage, it's not very satisfactory, but the piano is a Bech-
> stein, a beautiful instrument to have. So now I have a piano to play
> and I'm not sure how to use it in the future . . . At some point we
> need to discuss this. I have some pre-composed music – but I'm not
> sure if I can recapture our improvisations on my own. Anyway we
> shall see.'

My head was still reeling from the implications of his decision to buy a piano,
when he took me completely by surprise:

> 'You look tired. Why don't you sit down and I will play you something?'

This was the most extraordinary thing anyone had said to me during my
career as a music therapist. While I had experienced occasions when a client
would play alone, I had become accustomed, in the main, to being an active
part of the music-making. Never before had a client suggested that he improvise totally alone, and what felt even more significant was the implication that
the music would be improvised specifically for me. This statement, I felt,
suggested a challenge to the roles of client and therapist. Quite what the
consequences of this would be, I was not sure. My shock paralysed any
coherent response. I sat down and he began to play. The content was dramatically different from our previous duets.

2 **Audio Extract Two – Session Three (2:53)**
- **Opening music.**
- **Tonal centre – E minor.**
- **The improvisation is initially based on a three-note cell (**  **).**

- The beginnings of melodic figures are incorporated within sparse two-part inventions. The music is quiet, simple and taut.
- There is an interplay between sixths and semitones:

- Octave single-line melodies emerge. There is a sense of floating.
- A section in octaves allows a sense of grounding. The music becomes momentarily faster.
- The cell now moves to E and F, the tonality touching on major keys before subsiding.

    (The improvisation continues for twelve minutes after the extract.)

The intensity of musical dialogue felt as though our preceding improvisations had been somewhat transient. At the end of the improvisation Francis asked me to reflect on the music:

> 'Tell me what you felt about the music.'
> 'Your improvising alone is different. The music was very sparse.'
> 'Yes. It depends on the word.'

His use of tension and resolution had impressed me:

> 'I had a strong feeling of tension with the semitone and the dichotomy between major and minor.'
> 'The improvisation was mostly on the white notes. I think I felt sparse, not into the warm romanticism of before. More a feeling of being isolated.'
> 'The music felt uncluttered.'
> 'The music was taut rather than tense. I was surprised at how I improvised alone . . . Playing with no input from you does rather change our roles in terms of what we have done before. I think that perhaps you become a kind of active listener. I would like further exploration in this way.'

My role as 'active listener' was to become an important dimension in the therapeutic relationship. There is no literature in music therapy concerning the therapist not partaking musically in the therapeutic process, although some authors (Bruscia 1987, Crocker 1957, Grinell 1980, Heimlich 1965, Nordoff and Robbins 1977) discuss music as a receptive medium, with the client in the listening role. Consequently there were no precedents to assist me in this dramatic shift of therapeutic emphasis and I could trust only my instincts that this was a necessary and natural development.[2]

Francis proposed that for the second improvisation we should return to the combination of piano four-hands, with me in the treble and him in the bass. In contrast to his solo, the improvisation was rich and full. This marked the first time that I recognized that he was deliberately challenging my musical ability. Unlike when facing his verbal confrontations, I felt confident and resolute. He had quickly become self-assured in his ability to improvise. This implied that it would be important for him to feel confident that I, as music therapist, would be able to match and reflect his music on a similar level. My role was developing a duality, on the one hand concerned essentially with musical components, and on the other with the therapeutic considerations of music. This view, I believe, is one of fundamental balance in music therapy: music as music or music as healing. It was one I needed to consider carefully in regard to his advanced musical skills. My thoughts were reflected in his next statement:

'When we improvise together in the sessions the expertise of your musical input is vital. I expect your musical inventions to be of the highest order, otherwise I would not be prepared to travel personally. I remember testing you musically when we first started working together – could you match my quite often intricate musical inventions? I needed that aesthetic musical content before I was ready to move on.'[3]

He looked directly at me throughout the above statement. I felt distinctly uncomfortable with the directness of his challenge. He then quickly turned to the keyboard and immediately began improvising in the bass as before. I waited for a moment before joining his playing, hoping that I could indeed provide the musical skills he so demanded.

[3] **Audio Extract Three – Session Three (4:38)**
(Ten minutes after the opening.)
- **Tonal centre C major.**
- **The music is quiet and subdued.**
- **A slow majestic pulse (tonal centre F) emerges, becoming faster with an increase in volume.**
- **The improvisation quietens to a section that is simple and clear in timbre. A simple accompaniment (bass) and melody (treble) evolve. A two-part invention is developed and extended between players.**
- **A further simple walking accompaniment (bass) allows a theme (treble) to be improvised:**

- **The bass announces a two-part theme in thirds:**

- **After a short pause there is a bridge-passage. The chords (bass) hint at less tonally centred parameters which are followed and sustained in the treble.**
- **A turbulent passage leads toward a structure that is tonally and rhythmically free.**
- **The music is complex and electrifying, culminating in chords that are fast, loud and atonal.**
- **A lack of rhythmic pulse allows yet further freedom of expression.**
     (The music continues for seven minutes after the extract.)

The improvisation concluded gently. Francis turned to me:

> 'That felt very different to my solo improvisation. I wonder what was going on in that statement? It was so full of life somehow, looking toward life rather than the more introvert expression of the first improvisation that I felt was more about possible loss and endings. Perhaps one complemented the other . . . ? I was also aware that there was a certain amount of testing, on my part, of your ability to improvise.'

The two improvisations in this session were pointers for the future, especially the decision by Francis to improvise alone. It was interesting that he did not explain if this choice was predetermined or spontaneous. Whatever the reason, I had the premonition that his solos would become an important part of our work. My problem was to assess how this link between shared and solo expression would contribute positively to the growth of our work. It felt not as though I was abandoning my role as music therapist, but rather that the relationship was being spontaneously heightened and enhanced.

In addition to the initiation of solo improvisations, Francis clearly challenged my musicality in this session. During my years as a music student my main commitment was to twentieth-century music and composition; along-side my academic work I also became involved with voluntary befriending. Becoming a music therapist fulfilled my wish to integrate both these aspects of my life. Francis set me a challenge during the second improvisation of this session that was one of the most exciting moments I had ever met. During my music therapy training I imagined being musically free and unrestrained in improvisation, recalling vividly the case study of Logan (Nordoff and Robbins 1977) and the inspiration I felt upon hearing music of such symphonic proportions. Here was a chance to achieve this ambition. After my initial feelings of fear, I rose to Francis's musical challenge with absolute passion. During this second improvisation, music and therapy became totally balanced and integrated. I was eager to continue the work and anticipated our next session.

SESSION FOUR – CONFRONTATION

On reflection, my response to the previous session was over-optimistic, as Francis entered the fourth session in a completely different mood:

'This is a bad day for me. I'm feeling quite tired. Tell me something encouraging and affirming . . . Tell me something about what I do?'

His whole demeanour had changed, the tone of his voice was impatient and his eyes betrayed a sense of pain that froze me to the core. I felt a total fraud because I could not see how to find a satisfactory answer. My reaction was to flounder:

'Your piano playing . . . the music . . . '

My words seemed to freeze as he stared, waiting for a response that would satisfy him. He was making it clear that it was my role as therapist to work with his feelings of chaos. My answer would have to be at least miraculous. It felt to be an impossible task and, after an extended pause, I spluttered out a half-hearted return question:

'Do you feel . . . ?'

He interrupted impatiently before I had a chance to finish my sentence:

'I asked *you* the question!'

My mind became totally repressed. It was preposterous that I couldn't formulate a simple coherent sentence that in some way would ease the situation. After a long, thoughtful pause, I ventured:

'Your music has grown.'
'Do you think so?'

His tone was still restless and challenging. I replied:

44

'At first your music seemed to cover up quite a lot.'
'Mm. Cover up what?'

His sharp and penetrating response did not encourage me to continue but did provide an opening:

'I don't know, perhaps you were trying to express something and now it feels a lot more direct.'
'I can't play in the same way on my upright piano, I'm still having problems in adapting. I have tried improvising on my own but it doesn't seem to work. It feels different . . . Perhaps it's being on my own. I don't have the same appreciation . . . Do you think I'm musical?'

Francis was desperately trying to fulfil some need. What was it that he wanted? Did he want me to praise his musical abilities? Did he need flattering? Numerous options flew round my head. The question seemed both illogical and absurd because surely he had felt the musical explosion of the last session? I was sure he knew how good his musical abilities were, and wondered if he was trying in some way to trick me:

'Of course I think you're musical.'

He responded promptly as if in some way I had made light of his suggestion, the tone of his voice sounding even more irritated:

'That's a *very* serious question as I have *huge* doubts. Huge insecurities about *even* having the right to play the piano. It goes back to my childhood, because of my parents. I had to fight for the right to play the piano. I feel insecure . . . That I'm not wasting the last few months of my life in doing something for which I have no talent. Or whether I have some talent that I could work on, which I have released. And so to find some other form of meaning . . . So do you think I'm musical?'

This questioning of his musical ability was at the heart of his anxiety. It had never occurred to me that he found it difficult to improvise or converse. He had always presented himself as confident and resolute. It was bewildering, therefore, to discover this underlying core of insecurity and doubt. Perhaps his feelings were a direct response to my musicianship? Could it be that he was frightened by my skill, hence the sudden lack of confidence in his own musical abilities? Knowing he would see beyond false flattery, I tried to answer the repetition of his question as sincerely as possible:

'I think that you are very musical.'
'Well, that's something.'
'You have a very creative spirit.'
'Do you think so? Do you think that I should work at that more? I always come up against other people's music and feel a barrier . . . I have

45

this problem with atonality. I don't think I express very atonally and it's
been a barrier, a constant nuisance to me.'
'Would you like to be able to play more atonally?'
'No, I don't think so, I don't want to do something that I don't do
instinctively. I think I get caught up in musical obligation sometimes. I
don't want to think in scales or modes. I don't want to think in domi-
nants or tonics either, which are similar to my problems with atonality. I
don't think in formalized and theoretical patterns, and it gives me a
problem because I think therefore I'm not really musical. This is cou-
pled with the fact that I can't sit down and play someone else's tune. I
can work out the melody but I can't harmonize it. I have a feeling there
is some musical creativity there, it's just not in that vein.'
'I can't do those things easily either. Does it matter? It's what you want
personally from expressing yourself.'
'Yes, I think our relationship makes a lot of sense . . . I would like to hear
some of our previous sessions. I think it might be important to get a
sense of playback because when I'm actually involved I'm not aware of
what I'm doing, so it would be good to hear it back and then perhaps
discuss it.'

As described earlier, it has always been my practice to make available taped
copies of sessions for clients to listen to either during sessions, or to take
home for self-analysis. Francis's request was appropriate and I hoped it
would restore his confidence in our work. The result of hearing improvisations outside sessions had often proved to be critical. Charles, another client I
worked with, stressed its importance:

'Listening at home, to the tapes we made, allowed me to explore what
was produced at various points during the sessions. This gave me an
insight into the way I was feeling and the way I interacted with other
people, depending on the environment I was exposed to during the
week. This facility of monitoring one's feelings has helped me to establish a balance, with the result that I am more able to tackle difficulties
that come my way.'

I was pleased that Francis had spontaneously raised this issue – and wondered how he might also reflect on the verbal confrontations at the beginning
of this session. He continued:

'I have moved from being quite emotionally violent to something more
sparse very quickly; a very different kind of style.'
'I feel that you are listening more acutely.'
'It felt like coming out.'
'Have the improvisations affected your life outside the sessions?'
'Yes, the affect was that I bought a piano . . . it's been traumatic . . . from a
sense of duty. Your confirmation made me realize that music therapy is

worthwhile . . . When, however, I actually acquired a piano it brought back all the previous problems of what I'm doing with my music, and do I actually have any talent. The sort of almost super-ego things with my parents, and the realization that I probably couldn't regain the level of virtuosity I had before. Once again I was giving something up at the same time as getting something back, albeit I was taking off in a new direction. It was within very limited circumstances. I had to stop thinking in certain shapes and forms and get back to thinking more directly in the here and now . . . what I'm doing now and not tomorrow.'

I had questioned the impact of music therapy on Francis outside the sessions quite instinctively. Perhaps after the opening challenges, I too needed verification that what we were doing was important. The insecurities and questions he had brought to the session were addressed in an extended monologue:

'Will I ever get to learn the Liszt B minor piano sonata? Will I ever get to learn it properly? I came up against all of these classic situations which was the reason for buying a piano. I am also having problems with adapting to an upright instrument. It's different from my association because my identification is with a grand piano. I'm creating sounds in a different position on an upright. It is a major difference. If only I could have acquired a grand piano and lived in a place where I could house one. So it's reactivated the difficulties in obtaining the music I needed as a child. The difficulty of expressing myself, of having to adapt to having a piano in my bedroom. Old issues have been activated and hopefully I will come to some sort of solution as time passes. My musical appreciation is much more profound now. Now after fifteen years I have a different level of understanding. Playing the Liszt sonata now is like watching television; I can sit down and read the notes without understanding. I approach it as an imposition, so to speak, I find this with other pieces I've played before. My musical understanding is at a much higher level. I'm not struggling to acquire the notes. On one level I'm struggling to play but on another I can look at it and play it all very easily and quickly.

'There's been ongoing work in my subconscious mind. I'm much more secure now about what I want and what I feel. So when I went to hear Pollini play in concert last week I was quite definite in my reading of his reading and feeling about his performance. There are the areas where there has been growth. I've played many pieces as a student from memory. I have memorized entire Haydn string quartets from the score for general musicianship. I had to learn about reading other instruments that I'd never played before.

'Improvisation is something you create and build. I remember listening to some Schumann and thinking "this is simply written-down improvisation". I mean he had an idea, he worked on it, he improvised around it and then wrote it down. That's how it came about I believe. It's a brilliant improvisation, that's all composing is. The line between improvisation and composition really ceases to exist, it's an ongoing process, particularly when we now have the technology to transcribe improvisations as you are doing in your research. With what we do in music therapy, the same still holds true. The improvisations we create are more than passing moments in time. They are compositions. Compositions of our existence portrayed through expansion and consolidation. They reflect a process that moves and develops towards a clarification of musical and therapeutic thought just as a pre-composed piece of music communicates to the collective listener.'

This assessment was inspirational for me. Since becoming a music therapist I had struggled with the balance between composition and improvisation, knowing that they were linked in the creative process. The view that improvisation in music therapy is essentially about assisting therapeutic objectives, thus more closely associated with the science of behaviour than music, is one that has always caused me concern. Discussing improvisation in its own terms is an aspect of music therapy that I feel is sadly neglected. Francis here expressed his belief that composition is essentially an extension of improvisation, and improvisation in music therapy is simply an extension of the creative processes associated with pre-composed music (Robbins 1993). Again, more of my beliefs about music and music therapy were clarified and articulated by the client.

We paused and I asked about his parents:

'Were there many expectations placed on you from your parents about music?'
'Not expectations. Denials and refusals. I wasn't allowed to study music as a child, it wasn't felt to be proper. So I didn't start studying music until I was over thirty. I needed to do it for myself. I finished the Guildhall in 1976 which was very late. I remember being at a flat in Westminster before I was able to study, where a young girl, she was studying at the Royal Academy of Music, played. I remember feeling extremely envious and thought, "I can play better than that if only I had the chance." Her playing was so academic, no feeling, absolutely correct; there wasn't a note or beat out of place. I felt so resentful. I remember that I used to get overwhelmed by music. I would try and obtain music that inspired me, or failing that I would try and write it down. I was possessed – it consumed me and I could do nothing about it.'

After these opening verbal explorations Francis asked to improvise alone. The music began with a melody in octaves developing into broad sweeping phrases in G major. A habanera-based rhythm (♩. ♪♪ ♩) subsided into a recapitulation of the opening theme. This improvisation felt controlled and concerned with aesthetics. The balance between music and therapy that he had discovered in his solo in the previous session was now avoided in favour of what seemed to be purely musical aims. He suggested we continue immediately with a piano-duet in which he took the bass and I the treble. The music was again very pianistic and masked by musical clichés. For me this music became frustrating and almost trite. It was as if his words had in some way detracted from his musical expression. At the end of the session he commented:

'I think we played well together. We had very fine detail within an enormously broad sweep – in the sense that I'm thinking of using a canvas that is broader. With the session as a whole I felt a certain sense of resolution. When I first arrived I was angry and I wanted you to provide support. I realize that it's a question of not fitting in with people's expectations and therefore feeling I have no value or meaning. This has been something that has followed me all my life, but never before have I been able to express it so clearly. These two improvisations have helped finally to put things in a clearer context through privacy [his solo] and mutual co-operation [our duet].'

As he left I promised to copy our first sessions from my DAT recordings on to audio cassette.

It was not surprising that Francis's feelings and interpretations were different to mine. This had been one of the most difficult sessions I had ever experienced. He had pushed me to the limits of my thinking and music. I remember contemplating that he might soon surpass me musically, and I certainly felt he had done this verbally. He demanded that I search my soul and respond with honesty and sincerity. It felt as though my whole being was under his intense glare. The outcome, however, seemed positive both for the therapeutic relationship and his musical expression. Despite this eventual resolution I do not think I have ever felt so pleased to come to the end of a session. My feelings were mixed: on one level relieved that I had survived the ordeal, but on another disappointed that my own sense of inadequacy was just as poignant as Francis's. During the week that followed I thought about the difficulties he had presented. Could I continue to be exposed to such intensity of pain and confusion? Where were our roles leading – if anywhere? Lastly, how would we find the equilibrium between music, therapy and growth necessary for our future sessions?

SESSION FIVE – EXPLORING BOUNDARIES

I entered session five with apprehension. Francis's disposition, however, was much more positive than I had anticipated:

'What would you like to do? It's all so exciting. Shall we start with a duet?'

He seemed to have completely forgotten the tensions and anxieties of the previous session and sounded enthusiastic about the potential task ahead:

'I would like to extend my usage of things musically. To explore the contrast more between musical restriction and freedom. I think I would initially like to play a duet based around A flat.'

This improvisation began with Francis in the treble playing powerful glissandi on the black notes, which then relaxed toward slow, quiet descending scales. As our music developed, a keen sense of listening and sharing connected us, the musical dialogue becoming consonant and lyrical. The improvisation lasted seven minutes, shorter than the approximately fifteen minutes they were averaging. It remained firmly within the stipulated bounds of the A flat. He spoke as soon as the music had ended:

'I'd like to play another piano duet, but this time totally free.'

The music began playfully, unfolding to a passage that was loud and rhapsodic. This improvisation was more expansive and lasted just over fifteen minutes:

'That was fun, it helped me express myself more accurately because of the boundaries set in the first improvisation. We played between organization and non-organization. It helped me to consider how boundaries establish meaning for the music itself and the therapeutic relationship. Boundaries are controlled by man and they can in themselves be controlling. You should be able to walk through them when you need or want to. It's the organization after chaos that is crucial, but chaos I feel is the creative component. Music encompasses and surrounds everything. It's the all-embracing medium that transposes the boundaries of human existence.'

Boundaries are necessary in all forms of therapy. They establish the groundrules that are essential for understanding and growth (Casement 1985). As in the therapeutic process, boundaries need to be adapted for each client's needs, the therapist reconsidering their significance as therapy develops. In music therapy boundaries become as complex as the process itself. They provide a framework that protects freedom of expression (Bunt 1994). In my ongoing counselling at Lighthouse the evaluation of boundaries was critical. I was often faced with situations that were new to me, in terms of clients' needs and my ability to meet them. It was important to be clear and honest about my feelings in order to safeguard both the therapy and my survival. This issue was further complicated by my belief that in music boundaries are different. The evaluation of music therapy is historically dependent on words derived from medical, psychological or psychoanalytic models. Through my own experience I began to realize that in music, boundaries become less clear and more multi-layered. Music and words are distinctly different modes of communication (Lee 1992).

Francis continued his enquiry:

'I wasn't concerned about playing together. In a sense I'm now taking that for granted. We are always together somehow. I'm not listening so carefully, so that one can allow things to happen, and they do. There is a calculation in the subconscious sense rather than the conscious. The union of the two people non-verbally, for me it's a complete revelation.'

The third improvisation was again a piano duet with Francis still in the treble:

'That was interesting. Very orchestral. For me it was less satisfying because our energy levels felt lower. We were still letting things happen, but it didn't reach the same climax and resolution.'

As Francis left I gave him the recordings of the previous sessions. It was interesting that he did not discuss the impact of listening outside the session until after session ten.

I was relieved. I had braced myself for a continuation of the testing of our previous meeting, and again felt as if I had passed a test. Maybe he would now be able to trust my abilities as a musician, therapist and human being with all the foibles and vulnerability they encompassed. I felt encouraged and more able to face the unforeseeable developments that lay ahead.

4

WRITTEN ON THE WIND –
SESSIONS SIX TO TEN

O divine music,
O stream of sound
In which the states of soul
Flow, surfacing and drowning
While we sit watching the bank
The mirrored world within, for
Mirror upon mirror mirrored is all the show,
O divine music,
Melt our hearts
Renew our love.
                Michael Tippett. *King Priam*, Act 3.

It was at this time that I began considering which clients I would approach to be included in my research. Having worked at Lighthouse for almost a year I was ready to begin the initial stages of data collection. My methodology would include evaluations from three individual clients, all of whom would be encouraged to take an active part in the research process. Francis was the first and most natural choice.

Developing the project led to an interest in the potential of learning more about music therapy through qualitative analysis. At first it was the musical content of improvisation that inspired me and so I concentrated on the parallels with music analysis (Lee 1989, 1990). This sometimes led to misunderstandings among colleagues who perceived this preoccupation as being unbalanced. Later in my doctoral thesis (Lee 1992) I tried to find equity through the inclusion of outside validators and more directly therapeutic indices. However, my preoccupation with music analysis was necessary in the music therapy relationship with Francis.

SESSION SIX – MUSIC, CREATIVITY AND THERAPY

Francis discussed with me his potential involvement in my research and the effect it might have on our work together:

'I feel very excited about the possibilities of being involved in your research. Even after five sessions I feel that I have travelled a great distance with accessing my musical self through improvisation, and how that in turn affects my personal state. I am beginning to get a clear picture in my mind about the connection between musical creativity and therapeutic outcome. These ideas I would love to have included in your thesis.'
'Do you think the research might affect our work?'

The question of including clients in research, a process that is very different from therapy, was an area I felt we needed to address. It was necessary to acknowledge that the research might act as a negative as well as positive force in our sessions. Francis, however, was single-minded in his determination to participate:

'I think for myself I am prepared to take the risk and become as involved as I can with your project. I think your research is potentially important and could have consequences for other people with HIV and AIDS. I know from our few weeks together that I feel changed in a way I never knew was possible. Expression through music could become a very important force for people coming to terms with their life and death.'

He proceeded to describe how he considered creating music to be the essence from which therapy developed naturally:

'One of the most important things for me is that I've never been aware of the fact that what we do together is therapy. We are making and expressing through music. I have never been conscious of a therapy situation in a sense that it is a stipulation that a therapy process needs to evolve. Of course, it naturally has done because of the inherent qualities in music and the nature of our relationship. It was an inevitable step. Our work is musically expressive and creative. It's supportive and contained while being totally free . . . I think I would like to play a solo.'

Apart from this discussion, the sixth session contained little verbal dialogue and was the first in which Francis began to shed his musical past. The single solo improvisation was based around four tones that included intervals of the semitone (a), fifth (b), octave (c) and diminished fifth (d):

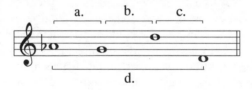

Francis at first explored the tones melodically, soon developing the framework to include simple harmony based around them. Heightened by semitones, the tone-colour became powerful with the inclusion of harmonic clusters:

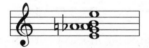

The idea of restricting the musical framework to a small group of tones was to become one of Francis's main improvisational devices. Known as the 'generative cell' in my research (Lee 1995), it developed to include melody, harmony, rhythm, structure and timbre. The careful choice of tones, normally between three and five, would usually be related to how he was feeling. The cell normally included the semitone, providing a tautness that allowed him the opportunity to include elements of musical uncertainty.

The improvisation illustrated, I felt, a clearer depiction of Francis's character. Coinciding with this clarity came a dramatic change of style that was both shocking and disturbing. He plunged into music that was tumultuous and violent, developing toward a peak of overwhelmingly powerful chords. I felt uncomfortable with what appeared to be this expression of chaos. After the climax his music became harmonically simpler, easing toward a passage that was melodically and pianistically simple. The improvisation closed with a coda that was quiet and evocative. Francis left the room in silence.

Reflecting on this improvisation, I felt his later expression of beauty and calm provided a balance with the bold opening. The depiction of opposites, which I have termed 'antithetical expression', could be seen as being crucial in allowing the contradictory sides of his personality to find expression. The distinction between the open nature of the semitone and the established major-key progressions was clear and balanced. This session was important as it was the first time that there was no musical contribution from me. Neither of us were prepared for this eventuality, although at the end of his improvisation I think we both realized there could be no more music. There was also the instinctive sense that verbal reflections would be superfluous.

Even though I had not actively partaken in the music, my presence had been important. Questions arose. How could I have been musically inactive and yet be equally absorbed? I had felt more than a spectator. Was the experience as much a part of me as it was of Francis? What was meant by 'being' with another person in music? How could music therapy be evaluated with the client being musically active and the therapist passive?[1] I recognized that Francis's musical inventions were becoming increasingly elaborate as the sessions progressed. This understanding, and the culmination of a single expression, aroused a sense of responsibility in me that needed exploring in my counselling.

SESSION SEVEN – PLATEAU

Session seven contained two improvisations: a piano duet, and a piano solo by Francis. Neither achieved the immediacy of the previous week. It felt as though our work had reached a plateau. In my experience this often occurs after a session of insight, and I saw this as being a natural consolidation for us both. The experience of a single improvisation in the previous session was not to become a regular occurrence until session eleven. The return to two improvisations in session seven made me speculate that session six had perhaps been transient. I wondered if the depth of expression latent in solo improvisation might have been too exposing at this stage. The reappearance of improvisations that included music-making from us both allowed Francis to share as well as to express alone. He initiated this return, leaving me to contemplate what other consequences might follow this initiative.

SESSION EIGHT – ASSESSMENT AND ANALYSIS

Francis's eighth and ninth sessions were held at City University, London. Here, I had access to two grand pianos, one of which was connected to a computer capable of producing accurate transcriptions of music played on it. I collected, in all, nine improvisations from three clients. This gave me a variety of improvisational musical texts from which I chose three to analyse in detail. In my dissertation I noted that:

> The change of location to the university, plus the knowledge that the sessions would be a part of the forthcoming research, created changes in the therapeutic alliance that could have had direct repercussions on the findings of the study. In real terms the improvisations appeared to be representative in terms of therapeutic development. The only differential, in my role as therapist, was a slightly greater concern with the musical elements (aesthetics) of the improvisations.
>
> (Lee 1992)

The three clients were then invited back to the university for individual assessment sessions in which to listen to two of their improvisations and comment on their content in relation to the ongoing experiences at London Lighthouse. These comments were recorded and transcribed. Three external validators – a music therapist, a musician, and a counsellor – also listened to the improvisations and provided assessment from their respective viewpoints. All this information, together with the musical transcripts, formed the basis for my overall evaluation of therapeutic processes in improvisation with people living with HIV and AIDS (Lee 1995).

The description of session eight will include information drawn from these two sources: the session itself and the assessment session. The sections of the assessment pertaining specifically to the improvisations will be included here, the rest of the evaluation being included in Chapter 5. I hope this dual illumination of the first improvisation will not unduly confuse the reader. Taking advantage of the resources of the university, Francis chose to focus a large majority of our improvisations during these two sessions on two pianos, interspersed with piano duets and solos.

The session itself

At the beginning Francis stated:

> 'I'm feeling quite hostile today. I thought I'd let you know beforehand
> . . . I may intersperse the improvisations with direct references to these
> feelings verbally . . . I would like to begin with a solo improvisation.'

The generative cell described earlier in this chapter took the central role in the musical development of this first improvisation. The three tones that made up the cell (A flat, G and E) were used in different combinations: in their original order, reversed, mixed, transposed and as the bases for harmonic forms, and intricately concealed within the overall structure. These complex variations seemed to suggest that Francis was conscious of the improvisational content and direction. The overall mood was sparse and bleak. There was a sense that his expression was held tightly within the cell. He spoke after the improvisation had ended:

> 'As always I'm searching for something.'
> 'Do you think the music reflected how you were feeling?'
> 'Yes. I have felt a lot of innate hostility the last few days. Internal
> hostility for all sorts of reasons. I'm dissatisfied with my environment. It
> helped me to place those feelings within a more positive context, in the
> sense that I could explore my feelings on a different plane. Expressing
> changes one's mood. The problem is the awareness of fatigue. Once you
> get in touch with feeling the unconscious, it breaks through the fatigue
> level. You can continue regardless and release further levels of energy.'

The assessment session

4 **Audio Extract Four – Session Eight (7:26)**
(Figure 3)

- Opening music.
- Tonal centre E minor.

- The improvisation is based on a cell (0:00) ( ).

- After an increase in tempo (0:53), a section in octaves (1:06) leads to a short chordal passage (1:51).
- A development of the cell (2:21) leads toward a theme that is clearly based in C major (3:35).
- After a passage of two-part octaves (4:03) there follow four sections of melody and accompaniment (4:58, 5:32, 6:30, 6:55).
- The music subsides to the core-note of the cell, E.

After hearing the recording of this improvisation which had begun with a clear repeated statement of the cell (0:00–0:20), Francis stated that while he became aware of the central role of the cell he was unaware that a complex cell-formula was developing:

> 'The cell for me is the closest representation of how I am feeling. It contains an intensity of expression that is both limited and expansive. This duality is crucial, though I am completely unaware of how complex the cell became in the overall make-up of what I consider to be these certain crucial improvisations. The cell thus provides me with a structure in which I can focus my feelings, particularly when exploring issues of death and dying.'[2]

He continued:

> 'I remember there, I felt, somewhat unusually, in a very downward mood. I remember saying at the beginning of the session that I felt hostile. It wasn't quite the right word . . . more a feeling of aggression. I was feeling that kind of dissatisfaction which comes from some confusion perhaps . . . from a loss of identity. Certainly a lot of my life has been a search for identity, in the sense that my family background didn't provide much opportunity for personal identity. One was being shaped into the British system, into which I did not fit because of my aspirations and feelings, which I now know were very different. I think when I don't have a strong sense of identity it can fall into some confusion. Then the confusion can make me feel hostile; I start tilting at windmills and become full of negative and critical thoughts which disturb one's balance. I remember here searching for an expression of moving down.'

Figure 3 Improvisation session eight – opening

59

I agreed:

> 'It felt very tight, very difficult to listen to.'
> 'Difficult in what sense?'
> 'Because the single-tones at the beginning were so carefully placed. I could actually feel . . .'
> '. . . the tension? . . .'
> '. . . absolutely.'

He paused, looked intently at me, and asked:

> 'Did you find it disturbing?'
> 'Perhaps disturbing is the wrong word. Unsettled rather than disturbing.'
> 'I think that was very much closer to what I was actually feeling. It's interesting that I was actually conveying that sense of being unsettled. The hostility I said which stems from a loss of identity, which is perhaps unsettled. I have felt a great lack in my life, in a sense that there is more likely to be a void or quicksand where there should be firm support. I say to myself, "there is nowhere to go, there is no one to turn to." So there was no security, nothing you could latch on to and say, "I'm safe." '

I felt his loneliness, yet with it the need to focus on the musical discussion:

> 'That feeling comes across in a very concentrated format in many of your improvisations.'
> 'That's good. I'm glad to get that sort of feedback because it means what I'm actually playing does communicate. It does mean something.'

He continued his discussion of the opening music by considering the relevance of specific tonal structures:

> 'The opening three tones are highly significant both musically and therapeutically. I work a great deal in what I would call cell unit-structures. These structures provide the musical boundaries through which I am able to express the deepest and most profound part of my psyche. The opening cell seemed to be the basis for catching something which was inexpressible. It was musically very ambiguous. I go in and out of major and minor a great deal also, this is because of the instability it creates. It takes away the feeling of certainty, inasmuch as you can on the piano. I have often felt that when I play something I have to bring in the element of uncertainty. I have got to leave the door open somehow. I mustn't say that is definitely there, it's suggested, it's half-open, it's glimpsed at. But as soon as you've caught it, it shies away, away again from the kind of feeling that is there.'

Francis was characterizing the generative cell in terms of his existence, revealing its essence in his music. The major/minor polarity also became an aspect of his improvisations that felt central to the dichotomy between security and uncertainty. This seemed to be a solo extension of the principle of antithetical expression. He continued the analysis by comparing a cell from another session:

'I remember in an earlier improvisation basing the music around three simple tones [he played to demonstrate]:

'The two intervals that were developed came out as a major second (a) and major third (b):

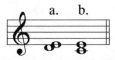

'The contrasts between that cell and the one I used in this improvisation are strikingly different in colour. This is because of the choice of tones and their different situations on the piano. It makes me realize the significance of your chosen keynotes, either consciously or subconsciously. How they will shape the construction of the improvisation is crucial. The therapeutic results of acknowledging and exploring the keynotes of your musical discourse cannot be underestimated.'

The first section of the improvisation had been stark in musical content and feeling. There was no inferred tonal centre and the harmonic searchings were kept strictly to the limits of the cell. After the overt passage of octaves (2:48), a tonal centre was implied as the music came to rest on repeated Cs (3:18). This quite unexpectedly evolved toward a clear section in C major (3:35–4:03).

I continued the evaluation:

'The long period of musical starkness. It was almost as if there was a longing for the major. I wasn't sure if you would give it. You did but in a very understated way.'

He replied:

'I remember a downward feeling, darkness and the longing for light. There's an almost counter-balance that out of this darkness light must emerge. But not too much light, just a glimpse.'

After another passage in octaves, this time a two-part invention (4:03–4:29) led toward themes based on a simple accompaniment in the right hand with the melody in the left (6:38–6:56). These passages were intertwined with linking themes based on the cell. The section (6:53–7:04) contained repeated arpeggiated major chords in the right hand intertwined with a descending melody in the left, again based on the cell. He commented:

'I seem to sense here a bringing together of the lightness and dark. I'm superimposing one on top of the other. They are coming together and then they are moving out from there into something else, something different.'

The improvisation continued to develop within the tonal relationships of the cell. It was not until the mid-point of the piece that I felt a release.

5 **Audio Extract Five – Session Eight (2:12)**
(Figure 4)
(Eleven minutes after the opening.)
- **Tonal centre E (minor).**
- **Fast-moving figures surround a theme based on the cell (11:58).**
- **A dual bridge-passage of detached phrases (12:25) and octaves (12:33), lead toward a more extended development of the initial fast-moving theme (12:51).**
- **This section descends with a trombone-like figure (13:27) and a long descending scale (13:46).**
  (The improvisation continues for seven minutes after the extract.)

Francis described this section:

'The whole passage is breaking up. Things which are emerging and then sort of getting lost and going away. I remember saying to myself, "don't hold on to it, let it go." It's breaking up, yet it is unified. The feeling of bottomlessness or instability is there, though the actual artistic production holds you. This is almost an idea of mine. You don't express the thing itself by being the thing itself. You express it and communicate it by providing a structure which in itself is supportive, even though you may be expressing things which are intrinsically not so. What I am getting at here is very much the feeling that all of this is being expressed and held. It is all being contained within an artistic shape which makes it possible for the listener to actually enter into it and not just fade away. I normally think in these terms: if you want to express boredom as an artistic feeling you cannot do that by simply boring the audience. You have to fascinate them by your demonstration of boredom so that they will understand its intrinsic meaning.'[3]

After this the music subsided towards a descending scale-passage of great clarity and tranquillity (13:46–14:07). He continued:

'I feel the whole improvisation has been moving towards this point.'

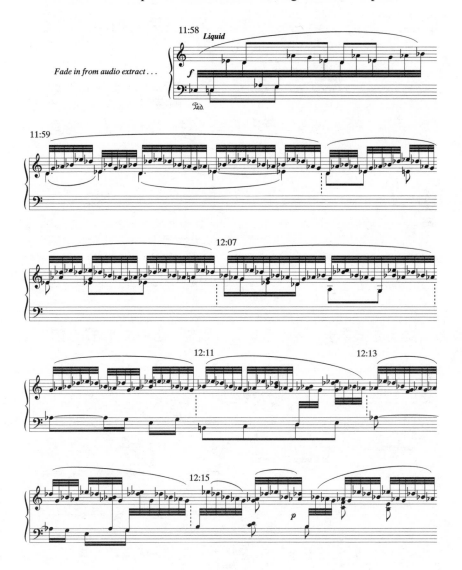

Figure 4   Improvisation session eight – development

68

I responded:

'I felt as though you didn't really mean it. You were almost jesting.'

His denial was adamant:

'*No!* I hear what you say, but *no!* That could be a *profound* misinterpretation. I understand that because of what you are seeing: it's incongruous, it's not for real, that kind of thing. You felt as though you were being taken for a ride or that I was joking. It's not that. Again it's the light trying to come through. The darkness and the light, all the way through and then for just that one moment the sky's clear. There's just that one brief moment when the clouds roll away. Then they soon come back in again.'

'I felt tantalised, like "Here it is, but you're not really going to have it".'

For a moment his tone became sarcastic:

'In that sense you wanted it to be something else, and I wasn't actually going to give you peace and tranquillity and "Happy days are here forever".'

He spoke forcefully:

'I was giving you a very powerful expression of suffering. In a sense it got eliminated – the most dynamic onrush of protest, pain and distress. After that there wasn't any room for that kind of sunshine. It almost is just to say that "I know that kind of harmony and light exists, it is something that one yearns for and therefore exists." How can you yearn for it, if it doesn't exist somewhere inside you! Therefore, for that one brief moment it was a part of my collective whole. It certainly wasn't teasing. You obviously must have felt deprived. You chose to feel and express teasing, which is critical in a sense, because you felt deprived. Perhaps you wanted something more and then suddenly I came back to you and you say "You've cheated me" – and therefore you say "You're teasing me." I wasn't teasing you at all because I'm expressing myself and I'm not trying to set you up. Of course there is the human problem. Your very existence can be a threat to someone else. The fact you say something can be felt by another essential being as a threat or something else. That is what we bring to a relationship.'

'I was feeling your pain. I'm not away from it. I felt this strong feeling that you showed me a chink of yourself and then quickly took it away.'

'You didn't embrace it, you stood apart from it and said "I've been had." Of course that wasn't the intention at all. It was a very brief moment.'

Francis's verbal explorations were no less penetrating, and the relationship we had begun with in the assessment session was changing. My role was becoming more confident. By questioning his musical sincerity I had unintentionally provoked him into defending his beliefs about how his music should be perceived. This was the first time I had confronted a client to this extent. By triggering his assessment of the musical experience I was pushing back my own limits of music therapy. His reaction demonstrated both his commitment to our relationship and his extraordinary ability to articulate his insight into musical expression. My reaction to his music enabled him to defend and consolidate his feelings.

We listened to the improvisation to its conclusion. There followed a long silence before he spoke:

> 'It's too much to talk about. What can you say? So much pain. It's a combination of pain and distress and anger and acceptance and refusal to be resigned about it. So much sense of purpose. Determination. So powerful. I don't know where I get the energy from. I don't feel ill afterwards. I always feel better and that's extraordinary.'

Spending one's working life as a music therapist is a journey of intuition and faith in the therapeutic process. Working in the areas of learning disabilities and mental illness one is often faced with clients who are unable to provide articulate responses about what is happening. We have to evaluate our work through various systems of assessment (Bruscia 1987, Nordoff and Robbins 1977, Oldfield 1993) so that therapeutic processes can be validated for future reference and growth. In the final analysis music therapists may never know the total impact of their work. Is it as pertinent or as powerful as we would like to believe? Indeed could it be even more influential? Working with articulate clients takes away these uncertainties. They tell you precisely what they are feeling and how effective you are in accommodating their needs. If the sessions are not effective the client will simply not return. During the year at Lighthouse I received both positive and negative comments about music therapy. Never had a client articulated as clearly as Francis how important the results were, both inside and outside the sessions. His comments were indeed extraordinary.

The session itself

The second improvisation took the form of a duet on two pianos. Through this instrumental fusion a more natural balance emerged in our relationship. In some ways it changed the roles of therapist and client to two musicians improvising. One could argue that this compromised the boundaries of music therapist and client. In my view, however, our interplay consolidated the music therapy process in a way that would have been impossible without this equality. I began to realize that music therapy is about two independent yet equal voices, sharing perceptions orientated toward the client, but also influenced and directly affected by the therapist. From my experience with other clients living with HIV and AIDS I developed a particular kind of therapeutic relationship that allowed a symmetry of musical dialogue. I began to address the possible therapeutic benefits of allowing the client, at certain crucial points within an improvisation, to support the therapist.[4]

In this improvisation the music was symphonic in proportion and content. The feeling of exhilaration grew as our playing became increasingly unified. The music ended triumphantly. Francis was elated:

'That was amazing. What comes to mind is that out of the chaos comes some kind of order. When order emerges you have a higher level of consciousness. The brain somehow is able to encompass the order that emerges. Therefore it allows it to become more conscious. It's a question of what the brain allows itself to perceive. The old Dionysian perception that what is known and ordered is beautiful, acceptable and praiseworthy. The chaos and violence of creating life is, on the other hand, improper. This improvisation, which allowed us the chance to improvise on two separate pianos, intensified the feelings that we have when playing the same keyboard. I think the physical aspect of playing our own instruments made a difference. I think, more importantly, it was the fact that we both had a complete musical palette from which to work. We don't have that experience when we are sharing the same instrument. It made a significant change.'

His enthusiasm continued:

'Through interplay you follow a consensus of what the best meaning is. I certainly never feel as though I must draw you out or impose my vision on you. We create a vision spontaneously together. The music has a life of its own. It's more than mirroring, it's some process of expressing. Of tapping into similar perceptions. A sense of identity. We are so close that we actually merge. We reached an apotheosis at the end of this improvisation. A moment of romantic affirmation. These moments do come; they are a form of happiness. We don't however always reach that level. You may be expressing despair or pain. Hurt or anger. You won't always hit that particular epiphany. But we certainly did today. This is the paradox of the ongoing process of enlightened experience.'

We seemed to have gained a greater understanding through improvising on two pianos, and through Francis's subsequent evaluation. The shared expression had obviously enriched the depth of our music-making.

Analysis of the opening improvisation had exposed the multi-layered complexity that lay beneath the surface of Francis's improvisations. The opportunity of accessing this information was critical in re-thinking my ideas. It proved conclusively that beneath the exterior layers of improvisation lay a veritable Pandora's Box of treasures, that could illuminate and clarify the enigmas of music therapy.

SESSION NINE – LIFE AND DEATH

Francis's second session held at City University included four improvisations. He requested that the first piece should take the form of a two-piano duet and that the musical boundaries should be restricted to white notes:

'That doesn't mean that I won't play a black note now and again!'[5]

The long improvisation is given here in its entirety.

6 **Audio Extract Six – Session Nine (19:16)**
- **Tonal centre moves between A and D minor.**
- **The improvisation opens with forceful question-and-answer exchanges. This theme returns in varying guises throughout the improvisation:**

- **The music is confident, with a sensitive combination of themes and colours.**
- **As the structure grows, phrases build, moderating to quiet slow passages.**
- **The improvisation begins to intensify, each climax becoming greater. Glissandi become important.**
- **A strong pulse (⁴/₄) leads to a quiet section that progresses towards further climaxes. Influences of Spanish music begin to infiltrate.**
- **The second section of the improvisation is based on opposing thematic ideas (antithetical expression). Fast syncopated octaves are placed against a fluid chordal progression. A strong rhythmic base remains.**

- The mood becomes frenzied. Chromatic (black) notes are heard. The rhythmic direction moves between structures that are free and regular.
- The improvisation becomes subdued. A slow coda with suspended chords brings the closing resolution in C major.

This improvisation contained themes of great sensibility. Though the content was at times complex, the overriding feeling for me was of mutual creative freedom. Any restraints imposed before were here overcome. The music developed through affirming passages juxtaposed with introvert reflective expression. We improvised music that was unified, balanced against music that was complete in its opposition:

'That was a very powerful statement. The music itself has an underlying thematic structure. I listen in amazement at the immensity of the composition, the overall grasp, the totality of experience. This is a complete major work that was just written on the wind. In contrast to other improvisations this has more obvious content, it is a wonderful demonstration of musicianship while touching on wells of feeling. There was an overall Spanish feeling for me even though the habanera rhythmic theme is not allowed to emerge as a definite idiom. It is just underlined somehow, unpremeditated and un-thought-of. There is a welling up as a result of our knowledge, experience and facility. It's a result of our personal and professional relationship, even though that was there from the start. It just flows and is so wonderfully elaborated. There is no obvious pathos. It's just there but also it's been lifted on to an artistic level. There are moments when things emerge very strongly as a total expression and other times when it's more hinted at. The music reflected . . . I'm not sure precisely what. I was looking for a kind of expansion, a feeling of expression . . . some melodic theme, some grandeur. I felt the need to bring in some blackness. I wanted a touch of evil, some more blatant discord. I wanted there to be some intrinsic darkness. I think the whole improvisation was very orchestral . . . in direct contradistinction to some of the more starker music we've had recently. It felt quite intense at times. A kind of intense overdrive.'

I was considering the improvisation's aesthetic content. It had felt as though I were part of a colossal structure, dependent on the musical framework while moving towards a greater balance between music and therapy. There was excitement at being part of an elaborate musical relationship that allowed my inventions to be both independent and shared. The musical content kept a fine balance between art and therapy, though it was my feeling that the intensity of personal meaning revealed a stronger connection with therapy than with art. Francis echoed my thoughts:

73

'I don't want to produce beautiful sounds. I want to sit down and find that it flows, means, has significance, value, and communicates with life. I want it to be a part of the life flow. Conversely, I cannot express myself through an inferior musical medium. I consider the musical content as being an equal and integral part of the music therapy process for me.'

The second and third improvisations of this session were no less critical. After the second, which was shorter, Francis had doubts about my participation:

'Not bad . . . do you think that was what you were searching for musically? I was playing something more dispassionate and I had the feeling that you weren't catching on to what I was playing. Your heart wasn't in it.'
'I think after the power of our first improvisation I felt as if it was difficult to attain a similar level of expression and so I became somewhat detached.'

He continued to needle me:

'Would you play a solo?'
'I'm not sure I want to.'
'I feel as though there is something you want to say.'

I had no choice but to acquiesce:

'I have never done this before but if you think it is a good idea I will try.'
'I do.'

This request reminded me of the confusion I had felt during Francis's challenge in session four and the surprise in session three when he decided to improvise alone. Again, I was unsure how best to respond. It felt as though he was putting me in the position of a client. My reaction was that this could be damaging to the therapeutic relationship. I had not been prepared for such an eventuality by my training and experience and so my response was guarded. Showing vulnerability within the therapeutic relationship has since become essential to my work in palliative care for it allows a balance to emerge between professional competency and human frailty. I have come to recognize that this is necessary in working with people whose thoughts are often focused on endings. Francis's challenge effected my first move towards conceding independent musical authority within the therapeutic relationship. I agreed, but with reluctance and hesitation.

My improvising was cumbersome, lacking any sense of individual creativity. The music became caught in extrovert clichés of warm romantic phrases. I intentionally hid behind this musical idiom so as to allow only minimal disclosure. The seven minutes' duration felt like seven hours. Francis was pleased with himself:

'Was that the lyricism you were looking for? I was feeling more soul in the Russian sense.'

I decided that rather than become involved with our apparent differences, I would offer him the opportunity to play a solo. The structure of his music was minimal, much of the improvisation being based on descending melodic themes. The harmonic content was simple, interwoven around a four-tone cell that acted as an anchor to which the music always returned. There was an intensity in the music that made me feel uneasy. After he had finished I felt prompted to speak:

'That was really painful to listen to.'
'There was mostly just a melody; the phrases always moving down. It was tense with pain.'

I could not but agree with him:

'I never thought a single-line melody could be so . . .'
'. . . emotionally and agonizingly direct?'
'Yes.'

His underlying sadness seemed somehow contained by his ability to express it:

'It's wonderful that it can be so communicative. I'm not perturbed that you find it thoroughly distressing because that was my intention . . . There are many semitones because they hold the dying feeling. I am just holding on to the vibrancy of pain. It was sparse. Very sad.'
'It had a theme.'
'Death and decay . . . Solitude and despair.'

These final words exploded in my mind. Francis spoke them with quiet intent, forcing us both to confront the realization that our work was ultimately about endings and death. Our examinations of music, our relationship, and aesthetics, were overshadowed by the stark reality of his impending decline. I remember sitting for what seemed an eternity in silence. Neither of us could break the spell these words had cast. Francis had spoken in spite of himself, his utterance welling up from deep within him. It was clear that neither of us could consider any further music. We both left the room in silence.

SESSION TEN – EXPRESSING THE PAIN

There was little talking in this session. I opened the brief discussion:

'How are you?'
'I haven't really been very well. I'm rather worn out . . . I would like to play a solo.'

The first improvisation wavered between loud, rhythmically free, fast music and quiet, slow, pulsed music. As the piece developed so these different styles were exaggerated. Francis's playing would become soft and lulling, then a corner would seem be turned and the music suddenly become startlingly different. His improvisation felt lost and directionless. I wondered if this was an attempt to keep a distance between us? Later, the improvisation again took an unexpected twist with short themes based around semitones. The music was harsh and violent, in a sense shocking to us both. At the end the music disintegrated with no formal ending.

After a long silence Francis began to weep uncontrollably. His crying contained a desperation I had never heard before. The air seemed tinged with his suffering. I remained apart from him, physically, during this period of grief. His crying eventually subsided. He spoke quietly:

'You play something please.'

I steadied myself and began playing simple open chords. My intention was to try and capture the pain he had so eloquently expressed, to improvise for him in a way that would maintain the intensity. I couldn't 'be' his despair, so I wanted musically to represent or mirror it. By trying to act as a channel I found myself capturing some of his musical ideas, balancing these with my own inventions. However, the warmth that was lacking in Francis's playing began to filter in, although it didn't seem to fit as I knew I was trying to 'make it better', desperately trying to ease his pain. I moved between what felt like musical representations of darkness and light. This imbalance between his music and mine became uncomfortable. I floundered to find a musical expression that was appropriate. Was it possible to allow this improvisation to be for Francis and myself, and for our relationship in therapy? As the piece developed I began to let go of these conscious thoughts and allowed the music to speak for itself. By relinquishing this expectation of failure, I was able to let the music find its own level. This style of reflective improvisation has come to form a significant part of my work with dying people, its core being taken from the ongoing relationship. By improvising for clients, attempting a reflection of their feelings and mine, I have found it possible to offer an emotional exchange.

The end of the session was as verbally compact as the opening. Francis spoke:

'Thank you . . . that's enough for today.'

We sat with our thoughts, parting silently to take our respective places in the world of words.

5

THIS WAS A PERSON, THIS WAS A FLAME – INTERLUDE

What I consider to be healing music does not necessarily avoid dissonances; it may well be fuelled by pain. But it is balanced by love. It may be blown by a crazy wind, but compassion is the rudder. It transforms slavery into shouting blues, oppression into the hard joy of free jazz. Healing music brings you in from the isolation of the wild to the companionship of the hearth, not through an idea, but through the sound of musicians who are themselves crossing over.

W. A. Mathieu, *The Musical Life*.

Between sessions ten and eleven Francis and I arranged time to discuss the improvisations transcribed at City University. Some of the material is contained in the previous chapter. Francis also spent time discussing music therapy generally. His statements deserve their own chapter as they consist of his detailed reflections on the first stage of our work. This gave me the opportunity to think about these and other aspects of practice that were important in the work with dying people. In setting forth Francis's thoughts this chapter will provide a context for the next stage in the therapy process. Its structure unfolds in the same sequence as the assessment itself.

NURTURE AND LOSS

Francis opened by trying to remember his initial feelings about our work:

'I've quite forgotten how we started. I'm trying to build up a picture in my mind. This is because of the fact that I'm tending to live very much in the moment and feel what I'm doing now. I have listened back to parts of the first sessions. It's funny that I can't seem to place their content in terms of our work. They seem strangely detached and second-hand. As if the music was played by someone else. I can't explain it.'

He became absorbed in what music therapy meant to him:

'I feel this is almost like a testament. It's the only expression I have of a spiritual journey. The only time that I feel that I am living and communicating. The only moment that I feel I'm living the time I have left is when I am improvising. The rest of the time I'm wondering what the hell I'm doing. Time is a limited factor. When I'm doing these sessions with you I am actually living a moment; I'm actually living with somebody and producing something and revealing myself. When I'm improvising, when we are improvising together, I feel that I am saying something and living – and it's terribly important to me.

'One has to balance the understanding that *nothing* is that important, with the realisation that *everything* is that important. That is the paradox. That nothing lasts and everything dies, and nothing can be the same again. The only reality is the moment you are actually living. I have this inchoate feeling of actually leaving something behind which will say: "This was a person. This was a flame. A living being. There was expression." I think it's almost like that. I can't leave a written word behind, and it's almost a sense of wanting to leave some kind of form behind.'

The need to appraise our relationship and Francis's wish to leave something tangible after his death were powerful affirmations of his explorations through music. His belief in expression through music, and the impact this had on his inner life, was a constant reminder of the efficacy of our work.

Feelings of loss and lack of support, which were to become central to the direction of session sixteen, were now touched upon:

'I remember an immediate sense of loss and frustration after the early improvisations. My own fantasies which come from my feelings of deprivation – of having to deal with endings and the destructiveness of others. This has been a problem in my life. It's dealing with what I have felt to be lack of support. Support for me as an individual, as a person – a value to be expressed both in my family and society.'

He was continually plagued by this lack of recognition, which often resulted in outbursts of rage. While he knew his musical skills and command of English were outstanding, I was aware of his need to be constantly supported and affirmed.

STRUCTURE AND CONTENT

Francis discussed the immediacy of improvisation in relation to the musical repertoire he had acquired:

'I've always had this fantasy of being able to sit down at a piano and produce beautiful sounds. I want my music to be a part of the life flow in a very spontaneous way . . . throwing away the restrictions of playing or interpreting other people's music; or being tied to any particular form or cultural tradition. One is working – even in one's immediate improvisation – one is inevitably working in that tradition. In a sense trying to express what is now and not repeat what was in the past. Not to search for something in the future, but to say, "This is what I am saying." I think it's that kind of flow that I want to feel. I want to be in touch with the living reality of expression at this very moment. Therefore it's music of today, even though I'm not aware of current trends. I brought myself up on the classical tradition. I think, as you know, that I have never been greatly enamoured of Beethoven or Bach or Brahms. I have always had a very personal perception of my music. It was initially bound up with Liszt, Ravel, Debussy and subsidiary forms, and some Prokofiev. That came closer to producing music that was of the day.'

A link between us was our interest in learning about improvisation through present-day music. I feel it is fundamental to relate contemporary music to the development of my improvisational skills; evaluating how different compositional approaches can potentially affect the therapeutic process. This ideology acknowledges music therapy as being a part of music's present and can have far-reaching consequences for our clients. The recent popularity of mystical pieces by such composers as Arvo Pärt and John Tavener, and the improvisational approaches of Keith Jarrett and Derek Bailey, can provide musical models and resources from which we can extend our musical components. By allowing new styles to emerge we open fresh avenues of exploration.

Francis went on to describe how he saw the individual components of an improvisation, or even a whole session, as being contained within a larger whole:

'In my improvisations I am trying to get in touch with myself as a living reality now. Rather than as a fantasy, dream, nostalgia or running away into something. I want to run *into* something, not away from something. I used to have dreams, I'd dream about being surrounded by grand pianos ... I never dreamt of an upright – one doesn't! ... of playing as we do now. What I do when I come here is that I have no idea what is going to happen or what I'm going to do. I think one of the reasons it's good to look back is because it seems that there has been change. At the same time I'm quite sure there has also been continuity. I'm quite sure there are many things that go on developing behind the scenes.

'I have a feeling that I had this initial tendency to think in terms of one, one whole. Now I've become aware of the fact that I see a whole in a larger unity of three or four parts. Not exactly sonata form, which I've always eschewed and disliked, but in the sense that I understand that there is a connection between having different movements. That you can fulfil an expression that will open up ineluctably, in the sense that it must follow – something else is waiting to be expressed as a result of what you have already expressed. There is that continuity of feeling that implies a change of feeling. Because you have expressed something and come to a temporary conclusion, like a colon or semi-colon, there is something to add to that. I think it does rather still put the first initial thing into the major position. At the moment that you let the first movement – for the lack of another phrase – remain the focus, the rest then follows. That is the core. It can therefore . . . I'm not sure whether it's a contrast or a feeling or the need to balance something, I don't know. It's more like the need to express something other, and then something other again perhaps. And yet this otherness is related to the first. There is a connection. Then there's a feeling at that moment, which is nearly always forty-five minutes or so – that is one total period – and then I say, "That is what I have to say at that stage."

'Leading on from that: I would say that in sessions with more than one improvisation, they are often intrinsically connected as if they are a part of one whole piece. There is a major statement – the first improvisation – which is then followed up by other movements: comments, feelings, remaining and resulting feelings, all of which complete a picture. Parts of musical expression don't exist in isolation. The major statement is surrounded by other things that are part of the entire colour scheme. With musical notation perhaps you would indicate a brief lyrical movement, which on the score would indicate another feeling. The lyrical loss quite often points to the chaos to come. A potential breakdown – an almost puppet-like poking, I think it's quite ballet-like. I see figures from *Commedia dell'arte*, puppet figures, jumping around, like a dance. Not of death, but some form of denial. Most sessions contain a whole life-cycle that is depicted, like life, through different experiences and expressions.'

Considering more tangible aspects of our work, he went on to discuss what might happen if the length of a session were to be more open-ended:

'I was wondering that if we think in terms of the music therapy hour, is one restricting oneself in some way? One could go on until you dropped from exhaustion. You could interleave with other people because they would set off feelings and then you could suddenly jump in. I had never envisaged myself in the group-work situation before. In reality, I think I would find it constricting . . . I'm just letting my thoughts run. It would become like a jazz session, I suppose, an endless jazz session. More things would well up and more things would come. As for me the hour never seems long enough. I realize the need for boundaries and the importance they hold for our work, though I could normally go on. I could start again and continue in some other way. I feel that I could get in touch with an almost endless flow of expression. This depends simply on my energy capacity which recently isn't always great.'

He was not the first client to suggest that the hour available for a session may not be long enough. It became such an issue with another client that I agreed to extend one session to two hours as an experiment. The additional time did allow us to enter into new realms of improvisational development, though it was, at the same time, exhausting for us both. The exhilaration from extended periods of playing may well offer a different cathartic experience. It is unusual, however, for music therapists to offer sessions longer than an hour, principally because of the practicalities of workload. Nevertheless, this approach could prove effective with certain clients and should not be overlooked.

SILENCE

Francis emphasized one of the most important aspects of music therapy:

> 'Silences are absolutely vital and shouldn't be shortened in any way. The actual length of a silence is the time that is necessary. It's the absorption period. Then I'm ready to, or I want to, or need to, move or play something to continue. That moment of silence is an intrinsic part. An intrinsic part of what went before and what is coming after. So it's absolutely essential that it should remain the same.'

In a letter to Chausson in 1893 Debussy wrote: 'Quite spontaneously, I have used silence as a means of expression. It is perhaps the only means of bringing into relief the emotional value of a phrase.' This could be equally applied to music therapy. Silence can highlight both the immediacies of the musical whole or of a significant moment. It may contain the apex of musical and therapeutic expression providing the mirror from which the music itself is reflected. There are as many different types of silences as there are therapeutic situations, each holding the potential for growth and assessment. Musically, Berendt (1985) discussed silence as a precursor to sound, and in terms of the therapeutic process Cox (1978) highlighted the shared silence between therapist and client as being possibly more effective than words.

In the terms of music therapy, Nordoff and Robbins (1977) discuss 'active silences' that remove tension, create openness and provide a sense of waiting. Here silence is an integrated part of activity and music-making. Priestley (1975) describes two types of what she terms powerful silence, before and after improvisations, saying, 'I think that it is in these times of silence that the being of the therapist most subtly affects the client' (Priestley 1975, p. 233). More recently, Bunt (1994) put forward the view that silence allows room and content to sound. In my view silence can be critical and should be given equal emphasis with music. One could further state that the cohesion between sound and silence is at the heart of an understanding of music therapy. Francis implied that to understand the implications of music, it is vital to consider the basis from which music begins and ends.

There are further aspects of silence that are relevant to this discussion. In his collection of essays entitled *Silence*, Cage made a point that was to have implications concerning my work with Francis: 'We need not fear these silences . . . ' (Cage 1968, p. 109). Throughout these initial sessions and the work that was to follow, silences became crucial. At first I dreaded their intensity, especially at the end of improvisations. It took me some time to accept them as creative, yet often shocking. Silences within improvisations acted as pauses, informing what had already been played and suggesting ways to move forward. They were carefully graded by Francis in his solos and instinctively placed in our duets. Silences became affirmations of music itself.

Understanding the connection between silence and death and dying is an important consideration for a music therapist working in palliative care. The silence holding impending death can express what cannot be said (Nuland 1994). Client and therapist must leave the man-made world of music and sound behind, accepting the spiritual dimensions of the dying process. Music becomes redundant in favour of the true essence of the relationship itself; two people 'stripped of their resources, as two human beings' (Sobell 1991, p. 148). Through personal experience I have found that it is possible to share the nature of that silent otherworldliness initiated through music. My initial discovery of this phenomenon caused me some bewilderment, but it has now become a central part of my work with dying clients. There is a sense that the music stops and the relationship continues. While this musical silence is almost paradoxical and impossible to quantify, it is one of the most real and spiritual encounters I have experienced.

TONALITY AND ATONALITY

In the opening chapter I discussed the importance of finding a balance between tonality and atonality in improvisation. During these initial sessions the harmonic emphasis shifted from strong tonality to a more fluid base, laying the middle ground between the two. It was rare for Francis to shed completely a tonal infrastructure. As he said:

'Tonality for me is the ability to use tones, within the framework of a consonant structure. Atonality is escaping entirely from that tonal system. There is always some inference of tonality in my music, I feel. Tonality forms the background from which most of my improvisations are created, any dissonance comes from within a tonal framework. The interesting thing is that I find there is often no clear distinction between the two. I often move between the two polarities without consciously interpreting my expression as being from one or either form. For me, the terms can be somewhat restricting and I prefer to think of my music as hovering between the two – reaching out and drawing inferences from each when my expression dictates. Leading on from that, it is rare for me personally to lose control, in the sense that I need to express complete irrationality. The specific feeling of being out of control for me can only be expressed through an atonal framework, in the sense that there is no purposeful key, meter, melody or harmonic sequence. This is a framework I don't often feel comfortable with unless absolutely necessary for my therapeutic bias.'

He examined the complex nature of the tonal–atonal balance and how, in his improvisations, there was normally some tonal foundation. It is interesting that he associated atonality with a sense of being out of control. It was rare, in my experience, for him to be completely out of control either musically or personally. That is not to say that freedom and loss of control are in any way synonymous: freedom can equally be expressed through consonant musical structures. Specific emotions and improvisational interpretation are more complicated and multi-dimensional than these interpretations might suggest. The loss of control in session three, audio extract three, highlighted the stark contrast between both styles of improvising, tonally and atonally.

CONSCIOUS AND UNCONSCIOUS ELEMENTS

The conscious and unconscious act of improvising has always been open to debate. Johnson-Laird (1991) stated that the essential psychological features are that musicians are not able rationally to articulate the process of their musical construction. He further explained his belief that we only have entry to certain parts of our minds and even less to our mental processes. An opposing semiotic view (Lortat-Jacob 1987) suggested that improvisation is mainly about awareness: 'improvisation brings into play a certain level of consciousness that may emerge as explicit indeed as verbal.' This idea was reinforced by Nattiez (1990), who quoted mainly ethnomusicological investigations to corroborate his claim that improvisation is based on well-defined models and the improviser's own physical routines.

Francis was able to discuss this from having lived it:

'Another thing that I have realized is that I have no idea of what I am going to play. Either at the beginning of an improvisation or during, I never have any idea at the time of what is coming next, I never say, "I want a major chord," I just play. This is the important thing. Looking back I can't say this note was an E, because I don't have what you might call the normal musician's perception of intervals and harmonic progressions. I don't think rationally. But I find what I want, this is the interesting thing. I have an idea of what I want and it just comes out. It's extraordinary. There is no conscious process. This is the amazing thing. I love it. This is what I dream of. When something like that happens and I see you smile, I think it's beautiful, it works, it's there and it's something that just happened. I didn't say, "I need a major chord," I needed an open sound. I needed to express something and that's what came out – and it was right and beautiful. Often, I think that the music is so carefully shaped. There is not a note out of place. How does this happen? I sit down and listen back to the improvisations now, I listen carefully and I'm amazed. I think this is wonderful. It's expressive and it flows. It sounds like a real composition. It sounds as though it was meant to be like that. Everything connects. Sometimes I feel that it goes beyond improvising somehow.'

In music therapy it is the unconscious material of improvisation that is critical to the therapeutic process and our understanding of it. Bruscia classifies the elements of improvisation in music therapy thus: 'Conscious components are those aspects of the improvisation that are kept in awareness and directed with purpose. Subconscious components may include anything that the improviser does not keep in awareness or direct purposeful intention' (Bruscia 1987, p. 563). Analytic music therapy (Priestley 1975, 1994) is based on the integrating balance between exploring conscious and unconscious states, music therapy techniques being applied to access each. It is the relationship between the two I believe that holds the enigmas music therapists strive so hard to unravel. The ability to describe or be aware of intended and spontaneous expression has been examined by Pavlicevic (1991) and myself (Lee 1992). While neither piece of research has classified clearly the connection between the two – where does consciousness end and unconsciousness begin? – the research raises questions as to the need to identify the musical and therapeutic consequences of each.

Francis described the process of being unaware as containing times of instinctive beauty. It was a constant source of inspiration to him that the improvisations seemed to have their own direction and structures. There appeared to be a connection between his instinctive need and musical result. As his skills developed, his music somehow transcended improvisational spontaneity towards a sense of pre-thought structure normally found in composition.

CHILDHOOD BARRIERS

Francis resented that he was deterred from playing the piano when he was young:

'It's all there because you have spent your life working on it, unbeknown to yourself. It's a part of your life. I started playing the piano late – I didn't start seriously until I was nearly thirty. I started from the beginning and then I stopped playing in 1976, and hadn't played since then until I sat down with you. I was right when I was a child and I wanted to play the piano, but I couldn't formulate and say, "I need to study music". Many people said that I didn't have talent and that I should be doing something else. My own instinct was that I wanted to play the piano, and I think it seems to me the facility which comes out when I'm playing is remarkable. After almost fifteen years without playing and I sit down and do that. I think it must mean something; I'm not struggling to put my fingers on notes. The very first day I just sat down – I talked to you about it – I said, "I think I've got a block, I haven't been able to play and I don't understand. I don't know why I'm not able to play. I can't find the answer." And I began improvising and suddenly everything took off. After all that time! If I had tried to play a piece of pre-composed music I probably wouldn't have had the technical capacity. When I'm improvising I don't worry about not being able to play, I just do it.'

The implications were serious, not least that his deprivation produced an ingrained block about his musical abilities. Improvising broke through the destructive negativism and allowed him freedom that was not concerned with his self-perceived lack of achievement and talent.

DUETS AND SOLOS

What are the differences in music therapy between piano duets and solos? This is an important discussion that can be highlighted by Francis's thoughts on the efficacy of solo expression, exploring why he felt unaccompanied improvisations to be more powerful than duets. Solo improvisations were to become the main focus of our later work. In our discussions I posed a central question:

'I was wondering about the fact that in your solo improvisations you seem to put in a different part of yourself than when we are playing together.'
'Yes, I have wondered about that too. I'm not sure, but on one level when I'm actually improvising alone, I'm entirely following my own internal rhythm and inspiration. When we are improvising together I pick up some of your rhythms and input. The sum of the two gives different results. It's almost a sense of how the tune gets changed in human lives by doing things together, rather than the increased energy input by supporting and solidarity. It seems that our improvisations together are more active, which I think is largely to do with interaction. You get a different level of feeling in the way you respond to people. I think I release some nervous energy that way. Duets are less of a personal document. They're less revelatory because if I'm working on my own it is a very personal statement. Music therapy I think depends foremost on making music, which in turn has a therapeutic result. The question for me is, why does a combined expression between client and therapist tell us less about what is going on than when I play alone?'

I offered:

'Perhaps you can't express yourself fully because there is the feeling that you have to, in some way, acknowledge and accommodate my music as well. What we do together for me is wonderful but I am aware it is not as clear as your solos.'

'They don't have the same personal quality. It would be interesting to spend more time, listening further to what the differences are in terms of the quality of music and therapeutic intent. For me the personal message is not so evident. With my solo improvisations more wells up from inside. It has a much stronger personal message. It's a very rich document of the individual self. When we play together we are working on a different level because there are two of us matching and playing together. Perhaps it takes more time to reach a co-ordinance on deeper emotional levels. When you are with other people you tend to express yourself at different levels in order to accommodate their company. Perhaps you are lost in some deeper feeling which you bring to a different level in order to accommodate the shared feeling, which is more immediately accessible. As you work together you can touch upon other veins. That may be a part of the difference.'

He continued:

'When there are the two of us improvising there is that element of musicality which comes in. Several different elements. One picks up the other person's perceptions, one latches on and is fed by the dialogue and enriched. The interplay of the two enhances in a sense that you are constantly having new material entering the musical arena. It's a dual process and it's a question also of the musical harmony. Of linking together the listening musical mind, and learning and being moved by another person's musicianship. When you are working together you express something which you don't on your own. You, in essence, create something rather different.

'The improvisations that allowed us to improvise on two pianos intensified the feelings that we have when playing the same keyboard. I think the physical aspect of playing our own instruments made a difference. Also, I think what is more important is that we both had a complete musical palette to work from, which we don't have when we are sharing the same instrument. It made a significant change I think. Improvising alone is an internal journey, one is in touch with oneself at that moment, one is expressing. Things emerge or well up and are expressed through the instrument that is purely one's own personal message. When I'm improvising alone I'm entirely following my own rhythm. My own inspiration. When you are working with someone else you can unlock different doors that wouldn't have been available on your own. When we are improvising together I pick up some of your rhythms. The sum of the two gives a different result: in a sense doing things together, rather than the increased energy by support and solidarity. Ultimately, I think that duets are less of a personal document. They are less revelatory because if I'm working on my own it's a very personal statement.'

The discovery of the significance of improvising alone was a spontaneous response. By relinquishing my role as an active participant in the music-making, I became an active listener at the most fundamental level.

THE CLIENT–THERAPIST RELATIONSHIP

Francis went on to discuss his views on the client–therapist relationship. He challenged me to consider my standing and how far I was prepared to travel in accommodating the emerging aims of our relationship:

'How far into feelings are you as the therapist willing to go? Obviously, when the client goes into feeling, how far does the therapist go, or does he remain on the edge of the field so to speak. Normally, one would not go with the client because it is not the therapist's role. In music, however, I believe it's different. What is one thing in verbal therapy, is different in music. If you are creating music then of course, if you hold back on your emotional participation, then you are going to fail. On the level of performance or productivity you say, "I'm going to put up a barrier, I'm not going to invade certain areas." Therefore you are going to control the situation and the client is not going enter certain areas, because he is restrained from doing so.'

I have found that the relationship with a client in music therapy who is facing death is different from other areas I have worked in. Why is this? Francis suggested that in music the therapist must allow a greater sense of vulnerability than in words. Is it possible that through a more intense musical exposure the therapist may achieve deeper levels of interchange and understanding? Musical unmasking and the process of dying then presuppose an almost double exposure for therapist and client. The impermanence of the alliance and the inevitable conclusion leave feelings that can be difficult. Perhaps these ideas in some way explain the power of the music therapy relationship in the face of death and dying.

FUTURE AIMS

At the end of the assessment session Francis and I agreed to formulate some aims for our ensuing work. These were:

– to refine further the musical components

- to consider verbal exchanges and how we might find an ongoing expressive balance between words and music
- to continue exploring issues of death and dying, when appropriate
- to continue recording sessions and for him to have the facility, on request, to re-access specific improvisations.

After we had decided upon these aims, the session ended abruptly. It was as if he had exhausted his evaluation or had become overwhelmed with tiredness. There was a sense of saturation, of completeness that blocked any further conversation.

CONCLUSION

The time spent with Francis on this assessment felt miraculous in its delving into the music therapy process. One of the fundamental strands throughout this book is the acknowledgement of Francis as teacher. This dynamic had never felt so real. His exploring of the intricacies of practice was confirmation of his inquiring mind and his fervour to attain greater musical and therapeutic heights. I had come to realize the importance he was placing on our work and how much it had already changed his life, and mine. The sense of responsibility arising from this took on a duality that formed the basis for my opposing feelings about our work. On one hand I felt privileged: privileged that I had been given the opportunity to work with such an articulate client. Accompanying this was the stress of constantly trying to achieve the standard of practice he so keenly demanded. It was this duality, in the sessions that followed, that kept me from consciously assessing the potential of our work. By shouldering the weight of Francis's needs, I hoped it might be possible to support and enable his further inquiry while keeping a sense of detachment necessary for my own survival. I viewed the sessions ahead with both excitement and apprehension.

6

EVERYTHING FADES – SESSIONS
ELEVEN TO EIGHTEEN

Music can never be abstraction, however thoughtful and objectless – for its object is the living man in time – nor can it be accidental, however improvised . . . because improvisation is not the expression of accident but rather of the accustomed yearnings, dreams and wisdom of our very soul.

Yehudi Menuhin, (1916 –) *Theme and Variations* (1972)

From session eleven onwards I was not to contribute musically again; my role became entirely that of active listener. There were fewer verbal explorations, the format of sessions moving toward a single improvisation, normally lasting between forty and fifty minutes. Music now took precedence. As Francis's illness became increasingly acute, his physical symptoms were ever more present.

LISTENING

Listening is at the heart of music therapy. Casement (1985), in presenting many examples of how analytic listening can direct psychotherapy, states that 'in trying to understand the patient, a therapist waits until he feels that he recognizes a thread of meaning that can be identified and interpreted' (p. 18). Through the therapist's listening clients are enabled to communicate their conditions and needs: 'limitless listening for detail, greater detail and still greater detail' (Cox 1978, p. 88). Cox also suggests that listening and empathy are innately interdependent. In music therapy the principle of waiting and listening, both at the beginning of and during the musical dialogue, is of paramount importance for the therapist's attunement.

The first music therapist to pay particular attention to listening was Pamela Steele (1988), who states that 'perhaps the most primary service which we offer our patients within the space and time of the therapeutic environment is our willingness and ability to listen.' She goes on to suggest: 'We have to be able to listen not only to sound, to the precise quality of a timbre, to the tone of a cry, to the placing in musical time of a single cymbal beat. We have also to be able to listen to the silences our patients make with us' (Steele 1988, p. 3). Tweedie (1979), whilst not a music therapist, encapsulates how listening can become all-embracing; 'The concert was lovely. Never, oh never, have I enjoyed music so much in my life! I became the sound, the music itself' (Tweedie 1979, p. 57).

Music and listening in society are inextricably linked (Storr 1992). In music therapy great significance is placed on the client's response: how the client listens and answers determines needs and future aims. Nordoff and Robbins have formulated responsiveness categories to different musical components and idioms (Bruscia 1987, Nordoff and Robbins 1965, 1977). More recently, Wigram (1993) and Moranto (1993a) have investigated the significance of the client's listening. With the advance of Guided Imagery and Music (GIM) (Bonny 1978, Bruscia 1991, 1995b), the client's role as listener has become heightened and, in regard to psychodynamic processes, specialized. The most important consideration asserts that listening does not necessarily equate with passivity. Listening can be as powerful a therapeutic medium as participation.

It is interesting that present-day music therapists, apart from GIM therapists, rarely put themselves in the position of sustained listening. My own awareness of the potentially wide role of listening in therapy was transformed through my work with Francis. The questions raised were important in determining how I would manage extended periods of stillness, in which I was not playing music. What of the music therapist as listener? How will his or her active stillness contribute to the understanding of music therapy? If music therapy and psychotherapy are allies, then why do psychotherapists view listening as essential to the therapeutic process and music therapists, for the most part, tend to play continuously during sessions? I have rarely heard examples of music therapy in which the therapist does not assume a leading role in the music-making. Are the elements of silent stillness and abandoning power in music therapy inextricably linked?

In considering music therapy with the dying, as Cox suggests (1978), listening and empathy are directly connected. By allowing one's mind to become open to the client's needs through contemplative stillness, both musical and verbal (Rinpoche 1992), it is possible that 'we might really begin to hear'. Listening forms the focal point of representation and meaning, allowing growth within the relationship throughout the dying process. Music thanatology (Schroeder-Sheker 1993) is a recent contribution to the use of music in palliative care. It is based solely on the client as a listener, receiving music at various stages throughout the dying process. The major difference between this work and music therapy is that the crux of music thanatology is not concerned with developing human relationships. It is about receiving a sense of musical purity, based on the chants of the Cluny monks, intended to ease and promote the dying process. Listening in music therapy is essentially different as it presupposes a relationship.

SESSION ELEVEN – RESTING PLACE

Francis entered the session solemnly:

> 'Last week I had a crisis that I expressed totally through music. Now I
> have moved onto a different level . . . I would like to play on my own . . .
> I'm not sure what's going to happen today.'

He began improvising with phrases based on the semitone and octave. The
meagre quality of the beginning then opened into a style that was warm and
romantic. This luxuriant music felt deceptive, perhaps because of his mood
when he arrived. The music moved toward a climax that was extrovert and
pianistic. Suddenly at the peak of expression, it stopped. A long silence followed that communicated feelings of being suspended. From this time
onward, I began to appreciate the significance of Francis's use of extended
silences. They acted as resting places, evaluating what had gone before and
what was to come. These times often heralded a change in direction. As his
solo improvisations became extended so the resting places took on greater
significance. There was something intrinsically powerful about these pauses: a
culmination of feeling expressed through stillness. They ranged from a few
fleeting moments to periods lasting anything up to three minutes. They were
always intense, and often painful to share. This improvisational approach
became increasingly important as our sessions developed.

After the resting place in this improvisation the music became simpler.
Francis improvised a pastiche passage in C minor. Another crescendo and
resting place led to what felt like the climax of the improvisation: a section
based on trills over dense minor chords. I began to feel less and less a part of
his inventions. His musical representations seemed illusory. There was a sense
of looking in on his expression rather than being connected with it. This
move to what felt like spectator status raised questions: had I always been on
the edge? Could I, indeed, expect to be anywhere else? It was again borne in
on me that my role as active listener had become crucial to our relationship. It
felt instinctively right, balanced with the concern that there were no reference
sources in the literature with which to evaluate what was happening. I had to
trust the moment and our developing relationship.

The improvisation subsided, ending suddenly. I began to consider the
breadth of Francis's exploration. Its length of forty minutes and its expanse
of communication seemed to have vastly extended the bounds available for us
both. Even though much of this music had not personally touched me, I
respected the way in which he had extended his musical and personal boundaries. The final silence lasted for what felt like an eternity. It was broken when
he spoke with quiet determination:

> 'Put that into words. I wonder whether it's really a good idea to ask
> what's happening. Maybe one should just let it happen . . . What do you
> think?'

'I think you are right . . . I don't have any words.'

'It was another move this week. So different ... words are so inadequate.'

Once again, we both left the session in silence.

SESSION TWELVE – FREEDOM

Francis again arrived in a sombre mood:

'My week's been difficult health-wise. I've got my local hospital organized which is very helpful to me if it works. They have told me what they can do and what they can't do. They have nurses who will come to the house. They offer terminal, convalescent, and respite care and have single rooms. I'm pleased to have the back-up sorted out. My diarrhoea can be chronic these days and they have helped me practically with that . . . I'd like to go to San Francisco for a holiday – I've never been there and I do like the States. I'd like to take some short holidays before it's too late.'

This was the first time that he spoke of feelings not directly associated with our work. A concern for his future care and the desire to travel, however, seemed natural responses to his deteriorating physical condition. He paused, his expression changing as he directed his thoughts toward the session:

'I haven't played the piano this week. I've been going through a deep sorting out of things, things that come into your head. There's an air of finality about things. Briefly, I feel that I've been arranging and sorting things out so that I can sit back and live these last months. Live them directly, because I've always worked through all the other thoughts and problems. So I can live directly from day to day and be in touch with what I'm doing – maintaining sources of pleasure in ever increasingly difficult circumstances. When you are no longer sure that you are going to enjoy a cup of tea, it's a little off-putting . . . I've a feeling of moving into the final stretch. I feel rather breathless today; however, I feel a lot more with it than I've felt for a long time. This is strange; I'm more able to look positively at the things I'm doing. The music last week felt released, very pianistic; there was a sheerness, a brilliance of pure piano sound . . . I'm really at a loss today . . . I need to play a solo.'

The improvisation opened with a simple melody full of pathos and sensitivity. I felt an immediate sense of empathy that had been missing the previous week. As the improvisation grew Francis began to use his resting places as a means of thematic construction. They became integral to the musical make-up. As soon as I experienced a sense of connection with his musical portrayal, the music would change, the texture becoming obviously pianistic. The improvisation developed; it became unsettling and macabre. I found it difficult to be alongside his display of overt showmanship. Moving on, he started to play clusters across the whole expanse of the piano, followed by stabbing syncopated atonal chords. I felt a sense of panic at this sudden expression of violence. Was this a more accurate expression of his feelings? After this sobering music, a playful, almost ragtime, idiom was introduced. I remember thinking, 'What is he hoping to achieve by this ridiculous change?' The style sounded hackneyed and without feeling. Toward the end he finally improvised music that was not dependent on clichés: simple, beautiful structures that were clear and lucid. The extended final section was slow and carefully measured.

As always, there was an extended silence at the end. Eventually, Francis spoke:

> 'In our society some people still believe that a lack of control means immaturity – this is just another way of controlling and eliminating opposition. In this improvisation I felt that I was losing touch with myself somehow: I *wanted* to lose control and not worry about the quality of the music I was making. I think that listening back I might be astonished at what I played, especially the section that was atonal. It is important to experience this feeling I think of being totally free . . . Interesting that I play for you but I can't improvise in the same way on my own.'

The ability to be free in music was always of great concern in my work at London Lighthouse. To be free from Western musical constraints is a difficult but crucial part of a music therapist's training. Clients at Lighthouse would often struggle to break from the bounds placed on them by inherited musical traditions. However, they often expressed their need for control by finding clichéd musical structures. Their fear was that by escaping from their known musical shackles they might also lose a sense of themselves. Most clients would reach out for freedom with apprehension. The clinical dilemma between this reality and the therapist's motivation to release them was a balance that needed handling with care. Despite any reservations I might have, however, when a client had an affirming experience of being musically free, it more often than not heralded a move forward in the therapeutic process.

SESSION THIRTEEN – CRISIS AND CHANGE

Francis's appearance now began to change noticeably. He was losing weight and his face became drawn and seemingly older. He walked determinedly and appeared to have difficulty swallowing. These were clear physical manifestations that he was dying. At the beginning of this session he revealed the extent of physical and mental deterioration:

'I'm not very inspired today. I'm very tired and I've got a headache . . . I feel very much at a loss . . . I'm very lost. I'm over-tired and depressed . . . I feel sad . . . I feel as though I'm losing touch with myself somehow.'

There was a long silence before he began to play.

7 **Audio Extract Seven – Session Thirteen (3:14)**
- **Opening music.**
- **Tonal centre G minor.**
- **Beginning of improvisation.**
- **The extract displays a simplicity of invention.**
- **The two sections are divided with a short resting place. In this instance, Francis uses the pause as a means to catch his breath before moving on.**
- **The music is simple and evocative, often improvised in two parts. It is based around the minor third; this interval being used as a cell for the melodic construction. There is a transparency of thought in the design.**
- **The texture becomes fuller, moving towards B flat major.**
- **A section based on melody and accompaniment leads towards music that is faster and more forceful.**
- **A theme emerges that can be traced from the opening music:**

- **The improvisation diminishes to a long pause.**
  (The music continues for forty-five minutes after the extract.)

The improvisation was balanced between two opposing styles: simple clear textures, as heard in the audio extract, and later complex trills and appoggiaturas. Francis went on to introduce a section based on scales and another in a pentatonic mode, returning throughout to the opening theme, which acted as a structural anchor for the piece as a whole. After the improvisation finished his mood was contemplative:

'The improvisation felt shorter than I think it was. I have a feeling that I'm getting in touch with a different, another person. I'm discovering the piano, but I'm also discovering myself. Because I had no feeling about what I was going to play today, I felt very dispirited and disillusioned. There was nowhere to go, I had no feeling about what I wanted to do. A chord or a sound: I didn't have anything. I felt empty, and it's remarkable the way something comes which is quite unconscious. I just get a feeling and then I carry on. I think the instinctive feeling is working faster – there's quicker switching, interactions and picking up of messages. The improvisation seemed short today, but it wasn't, which is very interesting. It also felt more articulated and direct. I think there's going to be a remarkable sound picture of a person's journey with AIDS. It changes constantly; it moves and reflects. There was a crisis point and then a change.'

My reactions to this session were diverse. When Francis had entered the room I had been shocked by his physical wasting. We had agreed from the outset to explore endings as part of the therapeutic process. What could I say, however, that would give him the space to address and express musically his impending death? Were these my worries rather than his? There felt a sense of refusal, that the experience of music somehow challenged what needed to be faced. One of my main concerns as a music therapist in palliative care was that I would work with the healthy, as well as the ill, parts of a client; that by allowing explorations of life and death, each could influence the other. Accepting death will in turn influence living; healing can take place when each is understood (Rinpoche 1992). As the sessions became more focused on living and dying, so more questions arose for us both. It felt that I had to learn to struggle for answers while acknowledging the power of realities that are ultimately unanswerable.

SESSION FOURTEEN – MAJOR AND MINOR

Francis's disposition seemed more positive. He strode into the room and immediately began talking:

'I had a lovely weekend at home. I feel a lot better this week. Perhaps it's because I'm getting things done . . . I have realized that it's wrong to think if you have AIDS that you are important. I've been very, very stupid. As a gay man I'm not important – and then to think that as a gay man with AIDS, that I could assume some importance to anyone is ridiculous. To be gay is to lose importance, and I've been labouring under this illusion that someone would think it's important and that someone would want to be involved. The reality is that no-one wants to be involved. People want to make money or make a career but they don't want to be involved. Once you've faced that it becomes very simple and things fall into place. What's the point of expecting something when the reality is very different? Therefore you can battle in different ways and try and deal with the real things in life. Like getting the best for yourself with AIDS.'

I was surprised that he had touched on these powerful issues so directly, including the bitterness of feeling that he was unimportant as a gay man with AIDS. My understanding of Francis was that he had always carried with him a profound sense of rejection. This appeared not necessarily to be connected with his sexuality or illness, but to his family and their acceptance of him. I felt that his internal struggle often mirrored his musical expression, at direct and subliminal levels. The intensity of his convictions and the influence that these feelings of exclusion were having on his life seemed important. In trying to understand his sense of isolation I reflected on the view that HIV and AIDS was a 'gay plague' (Shilts 1987) and the feelings of retribution that went hand in hand with this: that in some way AIDS was sent to purge the minority groups in society. In my experience, feelings of isolation come from an innate sense of hostility, a negative projection that had major implications for many people I worked with. Francis's statement encapsulated the view of many others. There was strength as well as sadness in his words. He paused before improvising, as if considering the significance of his words.

The improvisation was harmonically balanced between C major and C minor. It lasted twenty-five minutes in contrast to the fifty-minute span of single improvisations in the previous three sessions. As in session twelve, the music left me feeling bleak. In this improvisation Francis's musical language seemed distant, denying my existence as active listener. A noticeable difference was the lack of resting places: the music continued relentlessly throughout. At the end he sat quietly as usual, obviously considering his playing:

'A short improvisation I think . . . There was a dichotomy between major and minor which produced a natural ambiguity. It was as if you were getting a glimpse of something because you are not quite sure who you are. There was a light throwing a confusion of identity. A waking-up theme that was a completely different colour. I go in and out of major and minor a great deal; this is because of the instability it creates. It takes away the feeling of certainty, in as much as you can on the piano. I have often felt that when I play something I have to bring in the element of uncertainty. I have got to leave the door open somehow – I mustn't say it's definitely there. It's suggested, half-open and glimpsed at. As soon as you've caught it, it shies away, away again from that kind of feeling that is there.'

The major/minor symmetry became an aspect of his improvisations that was central in establishing a pivot between security and uncertainty. There has always been debate on the effects of major and minor triads in improvisation. In terms of analytical music therapy Priestley holds that 'major common chords soothe, strengthen and regularize while the minor chords ease sorrow and yearning' (Priestley 1975, p. 214). This argument would seem to be an oversimplification of the musical and therapeutic properties of major and minor triads and keys. Cooke (1959) explored the view that major equals pleasure, and minor equals sadness, but suggested that in other cultures the opposite may be true. In music therapy our perceptions of major or minor can have far-reaching consequences for the process itself. As Bunt stresses:

A careful study of harmonic implications, with all the interplay of tensions, dissonances, consonances and expectations, can further the music therapist's understanding of some of the most complex processes at work.

(Bunt 1994, p. 70)

Francis often used the juxtaposition of major and minor to promote ambiguity. In his playing, there was a sense that he had a creative impulse, realized it and then moved forward. Indecisiveness was often expressed in a balance of major and minor harmony and melody. He was not the only client to use this balance of harmonic and melodic emphasis. Two other clients at this time used the contrast between white-note modes and the pentatonic based on D flat to great effect.

SESSION FIFTEEN – DIRECT EXPRESSION

The improvisation in this session took another step forward. There was no opening dialogue other than a mutual greeting. Francis went to the piano and immediately began improvising. I was somewhat taken aback by this display of silent determination. My initial thoughts centred around how he was representing the continued sense of ambiguity so clearly displayed in the previous session. Extrovert, loud, atonal phrases in the bass were balanced against introvert, quiet, tonal voicings in the treble. The music felt significantly different from the previous session, less banal and more direct. His ongoing battle between light and dark was now clear and compelling. As the improvisation developed so the energy grew, revealing an aspect I had not seen before. The improvisation was a kind of wild piano concerto. I thought, 'What must Francis be feeling?' 'How can he find the strength to attain such fervency?' His extrovert and introvert playing took on a unity. Resting places became pivotal in effecting a balance of expression. The improvisation culminated in a section of carefully measured and beautifully structured music.

Francis's energy levels in creating music were growing even more intense. I felt honoured to be privy to what felt like a life-cycle portrayed through music. As the improvisation finally subsided I remember longing for calm – after such passion surely serenity must be the most appropriate ending. Francis, however, provided a backdrop of simple chords against which he carefully placed a succession of semitones and dissonances.

After a long silence he spoke:

'Time to stop . . . My energy levels are low . . .What did you think of the improvisation?'
'It felt like a symphony of your emotions. To me it was bleak and hard.'
'There wasn't much let-up was there? . . . I didn't want to let up. Why should I? I felt that after the crisis at the opening, the music became in one way more melodic and harmonic. More ordered . . . in many ways

97

than it used to be. It's an unconscious feeling of shapes and disconnected movements.'

'It had a calculated coldness.'

'It was the right thing to express. That is very much what I am feeling.
Coldness with the inevitability of death. The grave is very cold. I think
in that sense it was a good representation of my feelings. It was a direct
statement of expression.'

After these closing comments we allowed ourselves another extended silence,
both caught in a moment that was hard to abandon. After he left the room I
felt dazed. The canteen seemed chaotic and unbearable. All I could do was to
find a quiet corner of the building and sit. My emotions unravelled slowly
throughout the day.

SESSION SIXTEEN – MISTAKES AND ACCUSATIONS

The main feature of this session that was that I failed to record most of it.
I inadvertently placed the microphone lead into the headphone socket, and
did not realize my mistake until the end of the long first improvisation.
Francis's reaction could not have been worse. He stared at me disbeliev-
ingly before releasing a barrage of verbal abuse. It felt as if I was taking
part in some Ibsenesque drama that tore at my emotional defences. I knew
that my mistake was perfectly innocent, but he made me feel as if I had
committed the most heinous crime. He said he suspected me of being jeal-
ous of his musical abilities, and questioned my motives for being a music
therapist. These were painful accusations; as hard as I tried I could not but
take them personally. It was difficult to remain calm under these conditions, especially when he demanded that we repeat the session again so that
we might rectify my mistake. I knew that it would be a mistake to accept
this ultimatum. For the first time I began to realize the relevance of
boundaries that would provide me with a framework within which to assimilate my response. He had tested me to the extreme: my head would
burst if I did not leave at our allotted time. Taking a deep breath I explained that while I realized that not having his improvisation recorded was
a shock to him, the session would soon be over. I would have to leave at
our usual time to prepare myself for my clients after lunch. Francis was not
impressed. He said that if this was the case then he would at least like the
opportunity to play a short improvisation in the time left. I reluctantly agreed.

8 **Audio Extract Eight – Session Sixteen (2:06)**
(Five minutes after the opening.)

– **Tonal centre E minor.**
– **The music meanders in the form of a chromatic two-part invention. There is
a feeling of tension.**

- The two-part melody moves higher and higher, both parts eventually rising to the higher extremity of the keyboard. The tempo is rigid.
- After a climactic section the lower part begins to move downwards.
- The music becomes slower and quieter, subsiding via a diminuendo and decelerando.

     (The improvisation continues for three minutes after the extract.)

The improvisation was full of bitterness and blackness that became more intense as the music unfolded. Francis had subjected me to a verbal attack; now he was exposing me to a similar attack in music.

At the end of the ten-minute improvisation he stood, drawing himself to his full height:

'What was your motivation for not allowing the first improvisation to be recorded? It makes me realize that I have to come to terms with the fact that things go wrong, either deliberately or unconsciously. Is that because people want them to go wrong? I can't assimilate that properly and it's still with me on a level that is perhaps unnecessarily high. At the same time it's very important that I evaluate what I said. It was important for me to stay and say what I felt – in that sense it was therapy. I explored what I thought were the various possibilities so that I could carefully appreciate my feelings toward you as therapist. I needed to relate this situation to my sense of loss, that I felt there might be a sense of envy or an unconscious desire not to save what I was doing. By saying these things it was good for me because I didn't just walk out feeling hurt. This was a very valuable exercise. Very often in the past I would have walked away and felt hurt; I would have smothered it and kept it all to myself. During the improvisation I couldn't run away. I couldn't walk and so I sat there and started to talk to the piano. I kept my eyes closed because I was going to cry. It was a form of containment. I felt raw and painful, like a lesser aching scream. I wanted to create Francis's funeral. It was like a lament. It was almost in no-man's land – that I'm not able to leave, I'm not able to do anything. So the laceration was expressed. At one point I remember running out of notes at the top of the piano. That was the end psychologically, because in the end what is the boundary? The boundary is nothingness. It's moving beyond. There are sounds beyond that don't encompass the field of sound. It encompasses the limits of the piano. Within the limits of the human ear there are a whole range of sounds and colours outside to which the human ear is not suited. In the sense only at the limit, a false limit, one had to turn back. It also revealed the piano as a percussive

99

instrument. It was the moment stretching to the limit and beyond . . .
Everything fades away.'

I left with feelings of relief and confusion not unlike the experience of waking
from a nightmare. The rising two-part invention in his short improvisation
showed that Francis was able to push his boundaries further toward the
unknown.

SESSION SEVENTEEN – STRENGTHENING

Francis did not speak during this session. Arriving quietly, he sat at the piano
and intently surveyed the scope and breadth of the keyboard. For an instant I
thought he might speak as he looked searchingly into my face. Our eyes met
for a moment and I wondered if he was about to say something profound.
The instant passed and he looked down at the keyboard, improvising immediately. The music this time was based on four independent themes, suspended around anchor points. The experience was of clear musical language
and structure, every note having meaning and life: music that was beautifully
sparse yet impassioned, clearly shaped within an aesthetic framework. The
session was significant as a time for quiet working and consolidation.

SESSION EIGHTEEN – BARBARIAN BEAUTY

Francis again arrived with an air of quiet determination. His continued
physical decline, however, was a constant reminder of the inevitability of his
death. There were no words before the music. The improvisation contained
two major peaks. They were both frenetic, forming two sustained climaxes
that shaped the music as a whole. The improvisation leading to these events
appeared to be unfocused. The first peak developed unexpectedly from a
resting place.

9 | **Audio Extract Nine – Session Eighteen (2:45)**
(Twelve minutes after the opening.)
- **Tonal centres D flat and C.**
- **Quiet clusters are suspended. Much use is made of the sustaining pedal.**
- **The pulse becomes regular, based on black-note clusters of the keyboard
  (pentatonic).**
- **White-note clusters form a pivot between tonality and atonality.**
- **The rhythm accelerates, the overall texture becoming expansive and free.
  There is a sense of freedom and letting go.**
- **The improvisation stops suddenly, holding the sound clusters, which die away
  to nothing.**
  (The improvisation continues for a further thirty minutes.)

I felt exhilarated as the music became increasingly wild. The second peak was just as powerful and free as the first. It came at the end of the improvisation and finished the piece with a feeling of high resolution. The improvisation stopped abruptly and violently:

> 'What happened? . . . I'm amazed how I always find the energy. Before improvising I normally feel so dead – I can feel the strength oozing out of me . . . What I think I've noticed during the last two or three sessions is that I'm much less possessed by the intensity of pain. It seems to be on a slightly different level. There is something paradoxically I feel, something in the . . . in expressing something on the piano . . . it's such a positive . . . all the words are inadequate . . . I feel that I am alive, and that there is meaning when I'm able to express through music . . . I'm almost afraid to say how much our sessions mean to me, which is why I'm so upset if an improvisation isn't recorded. It's such a sense of loss as it's only once that I can say it in that particular form. It has taken on for me a sense that something will remain after I die.'

Having sessions recorded was something that Francis became more involved with as our work developed. It became a preoccupation that caused me some concern. I knew of music therapists who intentionally did not record, believing in the inherent immediacy of the moment. By recording I was able to reflect and make relevant comments that could be of help for following sessions. I also felt that Francis could use the recordings positively outside sessions. My fear was that the recordings might become more important than the musical experience itself. I considered the implications of this in my counselling. Why was I concerned? What might be the consequence of confronting Francis on this issue? The reality was that his beliefs were well founded and that his legacy would make an important contribution to music therapy.

He continued:

> 'I had something to say and never was able to say it in a traditional manner. It was never found until I started with you. I had always this dream of just sitting at the piano and expressing, free of preconceived programmes or other people's visions. I am still amazed that I do something every week and that I'm still able to do it. I did feel: how much longer will I be able to do this? Will I run out of steam or suddenly become extremely self-conscious and not be able to play? I thought, well, the best thing is not to think about it but just to let happen whatever happens. A bit like Judy Garland who went for voice training lessons. She thought she might lose her voice, which of course was quite the wrong thing for her kind of production and performance.'

He now began to discuss the intense extrovert sections of the improvisation:

'Beauty that has a kind of barbarian quality takes time to absorb. What is apparently ugly today will become beautiful tomorrow. If you try and erase ugliness for the sake of past beauty you are erasing your own creative function . . . There was a line of beauty emerging, it wasn't just a barrage of notes. There was shape, sound and light that came through. Words become inadequate, particularly when the words become fetishes or passwords for things. It constantly requires dredging up from one's soul – the right form of expression. It's a constant labour to create one's own language so that it says what one wants it to say . . . You cannot express in words what you express in music, they are different media. One can feed the other, but they are essentially different. I mean the word is the word and the word partakes of sound – in the sense that it partakes of sound and moves into poetry. Therefore it can blend and meet up with music in the sense that *it* uses sound and ambiguity of poetry. I believe it – in at once a more unconscious sense and a more inclusive sense. I see music as being at once straight into the unconscious feeling and inclusive practically of all other. It somehow encircles in its own non-verbalization.'

One of the themes of this book is my belief that expression through words and expression through music are essentially different. Francis's idea that poetry bridges this gap seemed logical. Berio in 'O King', from his composition 'Sinfonia' for voices and orchestra, developed an original musical construction based on phonetic fragments. The vowels contained in the words 'O Martin Luther King' are broken down and developed through mouth sounds set down by the International Phonetic Association. The increase in orchestral harmonic intensity is balanced against a phonetic mêlée that produces a profound balance between speech-parts and music (Osmond-Smith 1985). It was the scope of Berio's risk-taking in this piece that was to have a deep connection with our work at this time. There is no doubt of the emotional impact of words that are poetic in content and nature. The movement was written in memory of Martin Luther King, the simple incorporation of 'O' at the beginning adding an almost indefinable sadness. So the words speak because of who Martin Luther King was, the pain he suffered and what he achieved. The score itself contains some of the most original, complex and inspired twentieth-century music I have heard. The intertwining helped me to realize that there was indeed truth in Francis's vision. If, as Berio reveals, there is a bridge, it occurred to me that music therapists could investigate such compositions as 'Sinfonia' to help them to span the gap between words and music.

These sessions led into the next stage of our work. Francis had shed the influences of established composers and archetypal idioms in favour of his own style. My role as active listener was now confirmed, although the necessity of relinquishing my musical involvement was still not easy to accept. Why had he tested me so keenly if the result was my continued musical silence? I missed the challenge of meeting his creative musical thought, of being stretched within the scope of symphonic forms. But to share as a listener in another's creativity at a profound depth meant that our involvement must be equal, a dual expression that came from a single voice. During the next eight sessions the consequences became defined and clear.

7

SEARCHING FOR THE LIGHT – SESSIONS NINETEEN TO TWENTY-SIX

And as for art, then she could write with light,
A rational, surreal photography
Reconjuring a world in black and white –
A pond in a box, a table of sea.
I see her in the dark, writing with light.

> Douglas Dunn, *Elegies* –
> 'Writing with Light' (1985), p. 23

Looking back over Francis's solo improvisations I recognized that certain structural devices appeared to affect not only the music itself but the therapeutic outcome. One of these devices I identified as the 'tripartite idiom'. Examining improvisation in terms of beginning, middle and end can be compared with a semiotic approach to classical music: 'the argument being that there are specific attitudes to a work's beginning, its middle and its ending and these strategies are an important clue to the dramatic character of classical music' (Agawu 1991, p. 51). Hayes (1994) also identifies the law of triple-creation as being fundamental to the laws of music: 'The three creative forces are at work everywhere. Nothing is created without them and nothing has ever been, for every phenomenon, without exception, is inevitably a triad of forces, a trinity' (Hayes 1994, p. 3). There seemed to be a correlation. Francis's improvisations would contain a beginning (A: the material is stated), middle (B: the material is developed) and end (A: the material is recapitulated). Many improvisations would be realized within this form. How would the identification of such a process help me understand the expressive elements of our work? By balancing the issues of life contained within the music I saw the potential of communication through three distinct sections. The idea of improvisation being contained within the basic ABA framework helped me to explore further the connection between musical form and therapeutic outcome. Establishing and developing themes was an important part of Francis's improvising. He would sow the seed of an idea, usually a generative cell, which would then become a springboard for other ideas to develop. The cell, however, would never be totally lost. The final stages of improvisations or sessions would include a recapitulation that would create a natural balance to the structure of the piece as a whole. The significance of the tripartite idiom continued to develop as our work progressed.

From session twenty-one Francis began to give titles to certain improvisations. He would do this either at the end of an improvisation, listening back after the session, or during the course of the following week. Naming of improvisations had never previously occurred in my work, and I was therefore unsure how it would support the therapeutic process. Could the defining nature of a title detract from the open, impressionistic quality of the music itself? Ought the transience of improvisation be fixed by names at all? On the other hand, I saw the positive value of allowing Francis to place his expression within a conceptual framework that would give his music permanency outside the sessions. Entitling an improvisation somehow gave it a distinctiveness. Probably the most important aspect of this initiative was that it allowed Francis the opportunity to find an identity that epitomized his feelings.

Another development was his request to have the opportunity of listening back to his music directly after the session. I would leave him alone with the tape-recorder while I had lunch. Until this time he had eaten in the restaurant directly after our session, but as he became physically weaker so eating became more difficult. He was often distressed that most of the food available was unpalatable for him: even small amounts of spice would give him diarrhoea. It was his choice therefore to forgo food in favour of listening back to the session. As I left the room he would immediately become immersed in listening. When I returned he would normally still be in the same position; head bent, eyes closed, an intense expression of concentration on his face. There was a sense of continuation, as if the session did not formally end until after this period of listening. Although I knew that it would not be clinically appropriate to be present during these obviously significant periods of private evaluation, I often felt that I would have liked to stay.

I remember experiencing greater strength as a music therapist during this time. The path I had followed in working with people with HIV and AIDS had often been hopeless and painful, though tender and spiritual. At last I began to feel able to address the profound issues of life and death within a therapeutic context, although the musical and therapeutic paradox of complex simplicity was continually challenging. Counselling allowed me the time in which to explore more deeply my own fears of death and dying. I looked at my relationships with family and friends. How would I live if my life became limited? Who would become important in my life? How would I reconcile future hopes and fears when confronted with a shorter life-span? Experiences of loss also became significant in that I started to work with bereaved lovers and families. The death of a client is always traumatic. Whether one has known a person three years or three hours, the sense of finality and emptiness can be equally acute. Although experiences of death and dying became more frequent, I felt able to face the impermanence of my work as a music therapist. I also achieved a greater sense of composure in response to Francis's sessions.

SESSION NINETEEN – MOVING FORWARD

Francis seemed quiet and low in spirits as he entered the room. He said nothing, his fixed gaze somehow looking through and beyond me. He immediately began improvising, playing loud, fast octaves followed by short, detached repeated chords – music that felt impersonal and bland. After a session of great headway, such as we had had in session eighteen, I knew it was not unusual to experience a plateau. Here, however, the sense of stagnation was so powerful, that I began to look deeper. Was it impossible to recapture and build on the emotional climax of the previous session? How could Francis endure further extremes of bitterness? Was he allowing himself time to consolidate his feelings by withholding himself? It was difficult to understand what was happening to and within him. He would allow me near his passion only by degrees. Each time he shed a layer of protection he would follow this with expressions of apparent disapproval or obstruction. The improvisation in this session, for the most part, was contained within strict expressive limits that were repetitious and detached. As it drew to a close I remember considering how best to respond. After a short silence he spoke:

'That improvisation was more contained. What do you think?'

While the tone of his question was non-threatening, I realized that my answer would be influential in either continuing to shield his musical expression, or in confronting what seemed to be a denial of his true self. The word that came to my mind was 'pain'. I decided to use this word as clearly and simply as possible:

'I didn't feel the pain in the music that I felt from you at the beginning of the session.'

He paused before replying:

'There wasn't the pain in this improvisation . . . I had a feeling that I had almost made a conscious decision to give up the pain . . . I'm not quite sure what . . . just to let it go.'

Irrational emotions entered my thoughts. Did Francis mean that by letting go he was now preparing for death? Our music therapy journey felt far from over. There were times now when I would become obsessed with my meditative interpretations of his music and words. I did not want him to die and I did not want our sessions to end. I consciously repressed my vulnerability, seeing it as a negative force within our relationship. These feelings of what can only be described as irrationality returned often throughout this stage of our work. He continued:

106

'I feel that I am moving into a different dialectic. It seems to me that I am giving up certain cries of pain, despair and isolation in the wilderness. I've decided that they are echoing in the desert, and since no one is listening except myself . . . I have decided that it's . . . I don't know how to express it . . . I think it is a form of stopping trying to communicate, in certain ways . . . I haven't felt that I've been listened to and that my needs have been met. I can't see any way that I can do any more. I can't find any other way to try and so I think it's a form of . . . I don't feel resigned, saying "That is so". It's almost externalising those experiences for myself and no longer seeking to have them mirrored, echoed or have them reverberated outside myself. A great deal can be said by not following through. There is much meaning in leaving things suspended rather than bringing them to a reasonably expected conclusion.'

My anxiety began to subside during the silence that followed. On one level I was confused by Francis's searchings, but on another, certain they heralded a new degree of awareness. In this session the musical encounter felt secondary to his verbal inquiry. Would this imbalance continue? I couldn't imagine words acquiring greater significance than music. My thoughts during the following week focused on how best I might offer my skills as a music therapist if this shift were to become permanent. I couldn't help but feel a slight sense of disappointment if this were to be the case, whilst acknowledging that this was Francis's path and not mine. Our relationship was now secure enough to absorb any necessary change in therapeutic direction.

SESSION TWENTY – SPECULATION AND SPONTANEITY

Francis entered with a sense of expectancy in his demeanour. He looked at me intently and spoke:

'This is the end of questioning and doubt . . . I had a significant dream that I was trying to open an extra window in my room that initially wasn't there. Now in my dream there's an extra window where I want a window. I think I've solved that with the piano, that was the extra window. What we were doing, I think, was lacking this space.'

All I could do was to consider in awe the magnitude of this statement. After a silence he took up his thought again:

'My conception of the piano is that it is all one key, that every note is part and therefore related. That is the scale, the entire keyboard. This has been a stumbling block for me in terms of tonality and atonality; that both are related and inter-related. Each embraces the other and there are no inherent differences between the two. The polarities of tonality and atonality are embraced from our own interpretations rather than any intrinsic difference.'

'What a wonderful view!'

'Do you remember on one occasion I was searching for more notes on the piano. There weren't enough. I felt I needed a greater musical compass from which to work. Looking at the piano today it no longer strikes me as being big. It's partly a basic physical limitation of size that we have been dealing with. I wouldn't change the piano, however . . . all those notes . . .'

He began to improvise. The music was fast and syncopated:

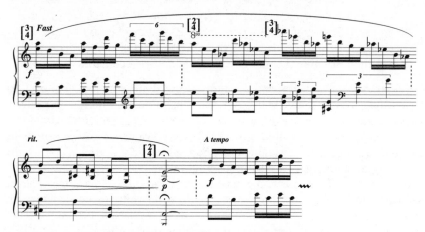

balanced against a hymn-like theme:[1]

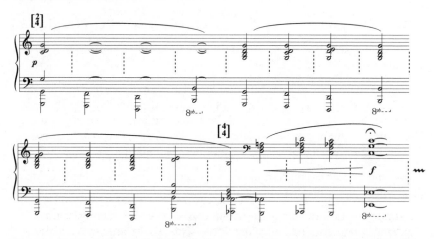

His playing jumped from idea to idea as the improvisation developed. Feelings of restlessness continued throughout. Clarity of expression finally surfaced in a section of slow minor chords. This carefully controlled coda formed the emotional backbone of the music. It was difficult as an active listener to hold on to any form of constant feeling. I was confused and unable to quantify my thoughts and perceptions. He finished with a great flourish of affirmation:

'There. That is it . . . I think there is a pattern, a continuity of movement. I felt there were variations on the light, a break in sessions – though you can't live twice, what happens, happens once and that can be, in a sense, a good thing. That you free yourself . . . I feel a lot freer. I don't feel even subconsciously tied to any particular line of development. I think I know that I have a fear that is irrational, of not being able to produce something if I don't have the past to lean on . . . though perhaps it's better to take the risk and just do where you are and say where you are regardless of wanting to. I think again it's the fear that leads one to try and establish principles – to establish some framework to hold on to instead of jumping in, swimming and trusting to God, so to speak, because He's greater than I am. If you're looking for props you are eventually going to invalidate your own creativity. So that one has to grasp one's freedom like a nettle and say, "I love you however painful you are." I'm trying to get myself ready for death in that I'm imposing a pattern on myself. I can die angry, why shouldn't I die angry? I don't have to die at peace . . . I think there is a difference in expressing an emotion when you are at one, than expressing an emotion when you are not . . . There now.'

The need to trust the moment no matter how chaotic it may be, and the view that one should have the right to die angry, felt both succinct and searching. These ideas were compatible with my own. I believe that a music therapist working with dying people has the fundamental responsibility to facilitate all levels of communication, no matter how painful or difficult these may be. Trying to place myself in Francis's position, I knew I too would be angry at having to die. The accepting phrase 'there now' became a verbal resting place. It was an extension of a sigh, a bridge between music and words. There was beauty in the tone of his voice as he uttered this phrase. He continued in the same introverted mood:

'There is a bitter-sweetness of life, darkness, light, pain, suffering, happiness, joy, love and anger . . . I felt a strong feel for the light . . . I'm beginning to wonder whether the analytic approach was more geared to a desperate attempt to survive an incomprehensible universe. By analysing things one could make more sense – much of my life has been spent on that, at the expense of my autonomous feeling and spontaneous creativity. This is the whole point of my creativity in our work. It is instinctive. I'm not using my critical factors at all – the English putting-down irony and sarcasm, that is so prevalent in our society at the expense of emotion, feeling and spontaneous demonstration of your perceptions. That is the creative, artistic part of one's nature. Analysis can be a defence, though of course there is a need for investigation and understanding. Essentially, synthesis is the road to wholeness or totality. Analysis must and can only be a part of the road that may help one with certain questions. It may also, however, hinder. I think if it becomes a barrier to expression or a wholeness of feeling, it then opens up an inability to give to one's feelings.'

He had raised the view that analysis addresses only one aspect of truth: considering this question for my research, I attempted to find a midpoint between quantitative and qualitative methodologies. By allowing freedom between these polarities I hoped to find a path that would address issues of both outcome and process. It was my belief that music therapy research should include the voice of both subject and researcher (Reason and Rowan, eds, 1981). Alongside this I felt it necessary to investigate empirical research orthodoxies that would add science to my artistic findings. This balance proved more complex than I anticipated. In adapting music analytic procedures there was a danger of losing the essence of the improvisation itself. My eventual model was one of form analysis that considered minutiae in relation to the whole (Lee 1992, 1995). Musical analysis was only significant if directly related to the therapeutic relationship. The final methodology was strongly influenced by Francis's views on analysis and creativity.

His music, as in the previous session, felt foggy and unclear, in comparison with his words which were precise and articulate. The music became superficial in a way that I felt revealed a sense of confusion. His words appeared to overshadow his musical expression. This stage remained difficult as I was unsure how best to meet his needs. How honest should I be about his apparent musical concealing? Not being musically active, I was unable to challenge him through improvisations. Musical confrontation was an important aspect of my work with other clients. A therapist can provoke through music in a way that is not possible through words. A resolving synthesis was denied me. As always I had to remain open to the changing balance of our relationship, however challenging it became. Francis continued to demand that I re-evaluate my assumptions about our work.

SESSION TWENTY-ONE – MONOLITH

My recollections of this session are vivid. Francis's opening comment was brief:

'I'm using a falling second as a leading-note in many of my improvisations.'

There was a long silence; he sat staring at the keyboard. Had he at last, perhaps, exhausted his possibilities in music? The silence was finally broken as he stretched his arms to the farthest extremities of the piano and carefully tolled the opening tones of the improvisation.

10 **Audio Extract Ten – Session Twenty-One (2:44)**

- **Opening music.**
- **Tonal centre A minor.**

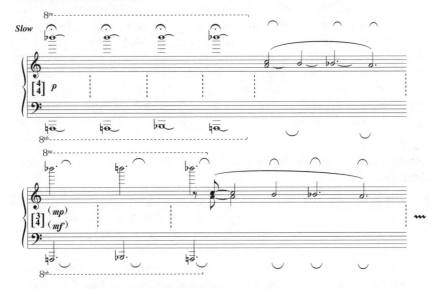

- **The improvisation is based around the semitone.**
- **Much use is made of silence and space.**
- **From an initial feeling of desolation the music gradually gains momentum.**
- **Small treble clusters are suspended, the music eventually resting on A:**

- **The chromaticism of the opening continues, retaining an intensity throughout.**

    (The improvisation continues for forty-five minutes after the extract.)

As he began playing I felt a chill run down my spine. I wanted to leave the room and his searing pain. How could he expect me to be near such carefully graded anguish? Looking toward the door I felt a compulsion to escape, but was unable to move. As I fought to keep a hold on my emotions the needs of the situation took over. Even though my feelings were of fear and confusion, I had to stay. There was the overriding awareness that this improvisation would be a painful disclosure for Francis. I felt overwhelmed. The fifty-minute improvisation remained huge and impenetrable, every note being carefully placed within the overall musical structure. Each note had its own meaning and life. The resounding opening theme became the cell to which the music returned with exactness and regularity. The tones seemed to hold the key to the suffering. Powerful extended silences unfolded that seemed to last a lifetime. There was an expansion in his depiction of beauty, an authenticity of communication that made me realize this was the most powerful improvi-sation I had ever heard. I wondered at the magnitude of his musical utter-ance. Images of blackness, death and dying went rushing through my mind. The expansive silence that ended the improvisation was broken by a few hushed comments:

> 'There now . . . there are no words . . . I think I would like to listen to that immediately.'

My feelings at the end of this session were diverse. It took many hours of intense reflection to place the improvisation within a secure personal and professional context. There were feelings of relief, the intensity of which had not been matched since the beginning of our work. After the improvisation, I wanted to leave the room and find a space where I could begin to make sense of this bruised yet tender music. The improvisation had felt like a barrage of emotions and sound. How was it possible to translate such intensities of inner life so clearly through music? Francis and I had explored the dichotomy of words and music, and the processes that allowed one to influence the other. His verbal precision and the mystical qualities of his music now seemed totally at one.

SESSION TWENTY-TWO – DEFINITION AND OPPOSITION

Francis began by attempting to shed light on the new direction of our work initiated during the previous session:

> 'I have found that by listening back to the music there is more musical shape and less emotional immediacy. I can remember some very strong feelings. They become, in a sense, transmuted and transmogrified into expression. Some of that immediacy is lost, which isn't a bad thing. There's less immediacy and more instant transformation into music. In listening to music and listening to therapy, it's not always easy to estab-lish the boundaries. I think in what I do there is very little pure therapy. It always comes out of the music, which is the best form of therapy.'

'The improvisation last week was the most powerful I had heard you play.'

'I think so too . . . I did feel that the piece was sombre and . . .'

'. . . monolithic?'

'Yes! . . . a *marvellous* expression! . . . I think that we should title the improvisation "Monolith" as it encapsulates the essence of the music and how I was feeling.'

'It moved me intensely.'

'There wasn't much let-up. I felt a great sense of containment, that unwittingly – in the real sense unwitting, without knowing – there was a preconceived pattern and framework that was the end. It was contained within the extremities of the piano.'

This is how the naming of improvisations began in this session. 'Monolith' came as a spontaneous reaction to Francis's music. I remember visualizing a black granite block that was impenetrable and immovable. His response to my suggestion made me realize that our relationship was continuing to deepen:

'There is so much one could do. One could almost put every moment into music. Perhaps it is artificial to have just one hour every week. What about all the other moments? It's all music and celestial harmonies . . . What was going through your mind during the music?'

'I felt intense searching.'

'I can't remember what I played. There was a different mood. The mood is related to my psychological search. Some kind of meaning or stability in these months. Hence, I think, the emergence of simpler or more tonal sounds. There is a kind of nostalgia allied to looking for an immediacy of expression . . . I don't think I really mean that . . . immediacy of expression . . . I don't think I do. It's more like a spontaneous expression that is actually in tune. There is a harmony between what I'm doing and what I want to do. I'm expressing what I feel or have mastery of. I'm conscious of a greater awareness in some ways in what I'm doing . . . But I still don't know what I'm going to do until it's been done . . . in the sense that I'm not leading. Something else is leading . . . I wasn't initially fully aware of how monolithic the music was. I was consciously trying to embrace the whole instrument.'

As Francis paused I felt a great sense of awe. He was grappling with the essence of communication through music, looking beyond the man-made qualities of sound toward perceptions that encompassed creativity, music and life in their most pure and embryonic form:

'What's happening at the moment is that I'm closing down in certain areas, but that I'm aware of the fact that closing down doesn't necessarily mean closing up. It's almost like a recognition of some kind of

113

reality . . . but it's not that . . . and that of course is unknown territory . . .
I'm living now from day to day, and what I'm making of my life *now* . . .
it's searching still . . . so in that sense, I'm not entirely giving up. However
much I say, "I put an end to that . . . it's a full-stop there", there is more.
It can even be interpreted as a gathering of strength. It's painful and so
easy to associate with loss and endings.'

The pain in his voice revealed that he was now facing death. The unity that
embraced us came from a spirituality arising from suffering and grief. As his
physical life was diminishing so his musical spirit was flourishing. Inner
musical growth and outer physical deterioration are aspects of working with
dying people that never cease to amaze me. Through this mystery I began to
consider the opposing perspectives of musical creation and dying. It felt as
if Francis was mourning. We needed time to reflect on the stature of his
music:

'I've been sleeping a great deal . . . I have an unsettled stomach. How do
you express that on the piano ? . . . there now.'

The tone of Francis's voice was slow and lethargic, as if the smallest utter-
ance would require the greatest effort. He began improvising. The music
lacked the clarity of the last session's monolith. The harmony was tonal and
the style of playing overtly pianistic. The structure of the improvisation was
based on two similar themes that remained unaltered throughout. The plateau that followed the dynamic experience of the previous session again
appeared as an inevitable part of the therapeutic process. He commented as
soon as the music had finished:

'I think it's a kind of intensity that I had last week, but not this week . . .
I didn't allow myself . . . I think that the music makes few demands on
you, the listener. I'm not sure why the music was so banal this week,
when last week the improvisation was perhaps the most important
music I had ever improvised. I think I reached a stage that was so
powerful that it was impossible to recapture or go on from that. Instead
I needed to improvise something totally opposing. Almost shallow I
think . . . I don't feel the need to hear that.'

We closed the session, parting spontaneously, with no formal farewells.

SESSION TWENTY-THREE – HARMONY OF THE SPHERES

This session moved beyond the plateau. Francis entered as if in pain. I
thought that it might be necessary for me to support him as he moved toward
the piano. When he came to rest on the piano-stool he released an enormous
sigh:

'I really am getting much worse. I have difficult eating problems and I

114

am so tired. I spend so much time sleeping that it becomes more and more difficult to keep going.'

I could find no words. We both sat in silence, wrestling with our feelings of helplessness. The thought of his death was incomprehensible to me. Our sessions had become such a total part of my life. Our relationship had changed my work as a music therapist, my knowledge and perceptions of death and dying and, not less, my personal life. As I let my thoughts flow freely, he began to play. The improvisation immediately captured the intensity of the monolith, though now the music was sensitive and delicate. The inspirational source of the music had changed, allowing me to relax and be totally involved in his expression.

| 11 | **Audio Extract Eleven – Session Twenty-Three (4:43)**

- **Opening music.**
- **Tonal centre A flat major.**
- **Arpeggios and broken chords move slowly forward.**
- **Small melodic motives appear from within the texture.**
- **The improvisation becomes impassioned.**
- **A resting place is followed by more atonally centred chords. This challenges the harmonic security of the opening.**
- **A chord sequence is improvised in F minor.**
- **A march-like figure in E minor is introduced briefly.**
        (The music continues for fifty minutes after the extract.)

As the improvisation developed so the music became more finely shaped. The clarity of invention was reminiscent of Beethoven's late string quartets. A few notes seemed to contain the depth of his meditation:

'What was I doing today?'
'Monolith part two I think.'

He paused:

'Mm, yes . . . It's something to do with creation I think . . . the harmony of the spheres.'
'Listening to your improvisation was like being a part of a waking dream.'
'Yes . . . What is reality? . . . That is getting closer to what you really are and all the manipulative symbols one lives through. I'm expressing the way that I would rarefy or objectify the world. It's the song that emerges from the different elements that have played on my soul. I think it's partly a striving to express one's own inner sense of harmony and

beauty. This expression also reflects the knocks, destruction and pain that distort that very basic life-giving feeling of expansion, the ability to feel what's going on around one. Is there an inner harmony which one strives for? Can one get into harmony with outer reality? Is that sometimes part of the struggle? That we . . . the gap between the outer and inner is so great. The difference between the imposed world of inherited values is so distant from the life-giving force, that wells up within you. This leads to jarring, destruction and violence. I think that when one is in touch with the creative flow, the life-flow within art . . . creation isn't a form of compensation or waking up . . . I think you can latch on to an inner message, almost like a genetic meaning that interprets the environment within the available language and tools. It's not just compensating form, it's something that hasn't been worked and wasn't there. I think that must define the lasting works which man creates – it is in touch with the river of life. The more you are out of harmony with your immediate environment . . . who is going to understand? . . . who is going to listen? . . . We should be in touch with our souls . . . So much is desperately time-wasting and energy-wasting. We spend our time tilting at windmills of our own creation, rather than turning to God's creation. I think it must be the need to externalize and evaluate, so that one can control, because one is afraid of the truth, instead of just allowing oneself to flow with the universal energy. It's the sin of pride, isn't it! It's hubris, wanting to create a power system where you can put everything in its place. By doing so you destroy the creative energy because you cannot contain it. Man cannot contain the universe, the universe contains man. We spend so much of our lives with these false values . . . with these power games – only admitting what you know and not being in touch with the unknown. Creating a barrier. Man makes himself so small by doing that.'

It felt as if his words had become a stream of consciousness. His music had accompanied him to this philosophical, ultimately theosophical, contemplation of the broader issues of life. It is unnecessary and inappropriate to attempt an interpretation of these words. They exist as a testament to the depth of his journey.

SESSION TWENTY-FOUR – DEVELOPING CLARITY

Francis entered in a quiet and serious mood. Apart from a few simple greetings he said only three words, and these at the end of the session. He stared down at the keyboard for his customary period of stillness before playing. The single improvisation was shorter than usual, lasting thirty minutes. It began with major chords and a simple melody. The structure was clear, fluctuating between slow simple melodies and fast complex passages. As the music developed so the level of intensity deepened. It seemed that from the beginning every note was meant and had a predetermined place within the overall improvisation. The music concluded with a slow single-line melody. At the end he looked directly at me and spoke softly:

'A beautiful ending.'

SESSION TWENTY-FIVE – COHESION AND FRAGMENTATION

Francis looked tired as he slowly entered the room:

'I've been sleeping a lot. There's nothing much else you can do. I had this melody running through my mind before I got here.'

From this theme, he began his improvisation:

He explored the intervals contained within the melody, modulating into C minor. Dissonances began to intrude. His playing had a meandering quality with little or no structural focus. As the piece continued, direction appeared, although the overall feeling of fragmentation and incoherence remained. His musical wandering had a sense of liberation and confusion:

'What was that about? It was quite a medley. I felt that rather than being carried along on one very main stream, I was picking up on all sorts of things which were shooting in from all sides and looking for space.'
'All the sections seemed equally weighted.'
'Yes. Each element had similar importance. That was very astute, in the sense that when you say it, it . . . somehow adds to what I did, and somehow pinpoints a major element. It is that equality of importance of all the elements rather than any one overriding the other. Even the more strident episodes were contained within the framework of the softer tones, and didn't take over or smother the other elements. They were stated on equal footing.'

In my working notes of this session I raised the following questions: I'm not sure what was going on in this improvisation. Am I on the same wavelength as Francis? I felt so detached. What was I doing? What exactly is my role? How does he see me? As a therapist? Or just a spectator? How is it that certain improvisations are all-consuming and yet this session left me feeling cold?

What does this say about music therapy, the relationship and the stage we have reached in the therapeutic process? So many questions.

SESSION TWENTY-SIX – THE CELL

The generative cell was now fundamental to Francis's improvisations. It was used at all levels: melodically, harmonically, rhythmically and texturally. He opened this session's improvisation with repetitions of a simple melodic cell in C minor:

The music became animated. Throughout the improvisation his expression was kept strictly within the three-note cell. Towards the end, the music moved towards C major and took on a liquid spirituality that had become the hallmark of his quieter and subdued explorations. The improvisation ended in its original key of C minor, inverting the cell with an ascending scale:

'I have a feeling more and more of expressing what I'm actually feeling. That I have worked out many things . . . I don't know how to express it . . . Many messages from the past. I'm looking more at things as I actually feel them. Using all of these elements but without necessarily carrying off the entire scene . . . I don't know quite how to express it. A balance of what I feel, and have felt. This is quite a good feeling. It's almost as if all of those elements are available for seeing life.'
'The improvisation felt very direct and precise. I felt very much a part of the expression . . . It's difficult to explain.'
'Yes, I understand. There are certain forms and expressions that bring you in more than others – you partake in different ways. It's like an inner connection, a direct connection with something that is innermost, conveying the meaning of being directly in touch with the elements, rather than having them filtered, flooded or trying to take control themselves. I found this week and last week similar in that balance. The music comes from a combination of nature and nurture. One has a creative instinct, and one has been exposed over the years consciously to musical idioms. They remain in the mind. It is I think very much an awareness of a heritage. I'm clearly expressing myself within a recognizable idiom which broadly speaking is the Western classical tradition. I'm certainly very deeply embedded, in the sense that I don't freak out into alien or oriental modes and structures.'

I agreed:

'Your style is now strongly reminiscent of you.'

'Yes, that supports the theory that the elements which you take in over a lifetime can be honed to become your own work. That can produce a style and context in which you can say: "That is now my moulding of feeling and thought, through the tools and experiences that I have assimilated and mastered in different ways." The things I have obviously responded to I am now making more and more my own – rather than just a pastiche or reminiscence, refined. The immediate connection is much more tenuous. The essence has now been distilled and the result is a refined spirit that is clearly synonymous of my emotions.'

8

AND STILL THROUGH THE PAIN I SAW THE RAIN – SESSIONS TWENTY-SEVEN TO TWENTY-NINE

Since I am coming to that holy room,
Where, with the quire of Saints for evermore,
I shall be made thy Music, as I come
I tune the instrument here at the door,
And what must I do then, think here before.
John Donne (1571? – 1631)
'Hymn to God my God in my sickness'

Working with dying people requires unconditional focus and honesty that can sometimes spread outside one's professional role. Although my contract at Lighthouse was to provide music therapy for one day each week, I became involved in other aspects of the organization's development. I felt my beliefs concerning oppression and the ensuing problems for people with HIV and AIDS warranted more commitment. In conjunction with Leslie Beck, the reflexologist, I initiated complementary therapist meetings and became a representative for the consultative forum, a panel consisting of staff and service users which met to review the services offered at Lighthouse. These extra undertakings happened gradually and added an extra dimension to my understanding of the clients' needs. It was these additional activities that led me to become a member of the organizing committee for the World AIDS Day Service to be held at Westminster Abbey on 1 December.

It was suggested that during the service a musical interlude, related to the issues of HIV and AIDS, would be appropriate. As responsibility for this part of the programme was given to me, I was drawn into considering the suitability of improvisations I had been transcribing for my research. Arranging a score from a music therapy session could provide very fitting music for live performance in the Abbey. The thought of being able to take an improvisation originating in an intimate musical relationship and recreating it in such a beautiful building was inspiring, though daunting. I imagined an orchestra capturing an intense climax, moving and inspiring the audience as they experienced the depth of expression realized by a client living with AIDS. I knew the improvisations from the sessions were musically dynamic, and believed them to be equal in content to compositions by present-day composers.

Ethical questions surfaced: was it right to make improvisations from music therapy sessions available to a wider audience? Would my preoccupation as a musician and composer usurp my role as a music therapist? Flights of musical romanticism were challenged as I contemplated the consequences such an event might have. It could be as dangerous as it could be enlightening for a client. I would need to consider carefully whom to invite to be a part of such a potentially explosive experience. Francis seemed the obvious choice: would he agree to be a part of the proceedings, and which of his improvisations would he wish to incorporate?

SESSION TWENTY-SEVEN – PERFORMANCE

For the most part, this session was taken up with discussing the possibility of arranging an improvisation for Westminster Abbey. I opened the conversation:

> 'I have been asked to supply music for the service at Westminster Abbey on December the 1st. It's World AIDS day.'
> 'Yes, I know.'
> 'It came to me that it might be possible to transcribe from my research one of your improvisations. This could then be used as a reflective musical interlude during the service.'
> 'Do you think that would be a good idea? . . . I'm overwhelmed that you would think my music good enough to be used in this way . . . I don't know what to say except yes – I would love it! It's what I've always dreamed of. Other people would hear what I am saying!'

I was delighted:

> 'We need to decide which of the transcribed improvisations to use and what instrumental combination would be best suited. There is a limited time-span of about ten minutes, so we will have to choose an appropriate section.'

Francis already had music in mind:

> 'My initial instinct is to choose the solo improvisation we discussed in depth in the assessment session, session eight, I think. I'm not sure where the first section ends, hopefully it fits within the time allowed.'
> 'Yes, I remember it, the improvisation based on the three-note cell.'
> 'I think it had an intensity of musical thought. I remember feeling focused and clear in my improvising. The tones I used were carefully placed. They portrayed my feelings of loss and searching . . . As to what combination we might use, I think I would like to keep it small. One or two instruments at the most.'

'Is there an instrument you feel particularly empathetic with that might depict the texture and feeling of the improvisation?'

'I have a particular affinity with the clarinet. I could hear the opening cell motive spoken through that instrument. Then perhaps just a piano . . . yes, the combination of clarinet and piano feels right.'

We began to consider the practicalities of the work that would need to be tackled. I would listen to the improvisation along with the score to find the first natural resting place. The section would have to end with a passage that made musical sense if the audience was to have any feeling of completion. We concluded by agreeing that if the chosen extract was the suitable length, I would bring the transcription along to the following session. He could then consider how best to score the music.

With this agreed, Francis sat at the piano and we turned our attention to the present session and to the day's music. His improvisation was based on a dialogue of semitones; it felt unclear in its direction and was shorter than usual, lasting twenty-five minutes. At the end he seemed perplexed:

'I don't know what happened. There is so much going around in my mind. The thought of having my music performed in Westminster Abbey . . . This whole concept has made it hard to concentrate on any-thing else. I felt as though I was looking at things but not taking them to their logical conclusions.'

Even though the musical content of the session was slight, it none the less felt significant. With the possibility of his music being performed in Westminster Abbey it was natural to have difficulty concentrating. On the surface I thought he had responded to the invitation calmly. It was not until the session had finished that I began to realize the full implications of my suggestion. Could a performance in Westminster Abbey in some way provide the confir-mation Francis had been so desperately seeking?

SESSION TWENTY-EIGHT – CONSTANT MOVEMENT, CONSTANT CREATION

Francis and I first spent time discussing the format of the music for Westmin-ster Abbey. There was a natural pause seven minutes into the improvisation that finished on the overall root note of E (see Figure 3) which provided a natural conclusion to the section. He went through the music mapping out the passages he felt most suitable for the clarinet; as he deliberated, I made notes on the score. A sense of excitement developed as his mind darted back and forth with ideas. He would decide on a combination, then reject it, be-coming increasingly impassioned as he realized the options available to him. This creative flow released a source of energy that I had not seen for many months. By the end of half an hour he had found an instrumental balance that seemed to please him. We agreed that I would transcribe the score as he wished and approach a student clarinettist to play the arrangement.

As he moved to the piano his demeanour changed completely:

'I'm feeling very much at the end of the road today. So little that one can do. I have begun to realize that I've been playing predominantly in G major and G minor . . . I've absolutely no . . . I don't know how to express this "end of the road" feeling.'

He paused, looking toward the floor, agonizingly lost for words. I felt useless, spontaneously wanting to hold him, to make things better. Eventually he began to play. It was as if we were both waiting, catching and holding his inmost feelings. I felt dread at what he might play but to my surprise the music was beautifully controlled and gentle.

|12| **Audio Extract Twelve – Session Twenty-Eight (2:10)**
- **Opening music.**
- **Tonal centre F minor.**
- **The music is simple and direct with liquid melodic figures. There is a clarity and control. Melodic lines come and go.**
- **After continued exploration of the opening theme the tempo increases.**
  (The improvisation continues for forty minutes after the extract.)

As the improvisation developed so the intensity built and subsided. His expression seemed to go beyond the reality of the notes themselves. The music acted as a veil. His 'end of the road feeling' was paradoxically symbolized within an expressive framework that was open and free. The improvisation ended in F major.

'Mm . . . I'm tired. I wonder if that expressed the way I was feeling. It seems to me that it probably did. It seemed to be fairly at one with what was happening . . . I did seem to be in my own mind, following my own feeling and mood. In a sense it was less concerned with . . . it didn't seem as though there was much effort put into pianistic work. It was quite a straightforward statement of . . . I don't know about the last section . . . I had this strange feeling of . . . I don't know how to express it . . . beyond the end of the road – and the road continues . . . something like that.'

I was moved by his mood of profound contemplation:

'The improvisation felt like an extension of the road somehow.'

He replied slowly and with considerable effort:

'There was this feeling of continuity at the end of the road. It's very hard to express. The road continues somehow, and it has to continue with a major sound. I suddenly felt at the end a need for a major chord, quite banal. It was opening out the sound. It's almost like an affirmation – one thing may come to an end – and the affirmation that life goes on. Behind and beyond the personal tragedy there is the continuum of life . . . A question of . . . In my story there is a feeling of having come to the end. A kind of statement of the . . . I can't express it . . . that life is there, that . . . yes, that life is there . . . And still through the pain I saw the rain. Beyond the immediate circumstances one sees something which requires the major rather than the minor.'

He stared at the keyboard and began to improvise again – simple major then minor chords. As he played I began to understand the synthesis of his words and music, how his free verbal interpretations had become almost musical and non-verbal in style. He explored his spoken sounds with an almost poetic clarity. As he moved from speaking to playing I felt the unification of his words and music. The improvisation lasted only a few minutes before he spoke again:

'The music naturally reverts to the minor. That's interesting. Perhaps it is just *too* open, banal and lacking in colour to express subtly of the moment. I can't go into optimism with a capital "O". There's light, but the light is tempered by reality. Circumstances, I suppose. That although there is the life force, and the beauty of life, the richness of feeling, it is inevitably touched by the instability and ephemeral nature of things . . . Life involves loss and death. Birth involves death, and nothing can be held on to. Everything is caught on the breeze – you can't hold on to anything. So there is an essential sadness in the very fact of earthly existence that brings in the blue notes that are the fabric of life. There are moments when everything conspires to produce a moment of co-equality into form, a momentary assumption of form that is held. There's beauty and then it dissolves and re-shapes into something a little different. Just occasionally we have the feeling of permanency – someone catches a moment that may be preserved for hundreds of thousands of years, of course, never I think, for ever. There are wonderful things that capture the moment of glory, they merge to produce simultaneous affirmation of glory and understanding. The remembrance of instability and change, constant movement, constant creation.'

REHEARSAL

Between sessions twenty-eight and twenty-nine I arranged time at City University to rehearse the music for Westminster Abbey. David, a young student clarinettist who had agreed to play, and I had a pre-rehearsal early that day. We went through the score to familiarize ourselves with the dialogue between the instruments. This initial mapping meant that during the rehearsal proper we would be prepared to concentrate on the intricacies of playing. Francis was due to arrive at the university after lunch. It was difficult to paint a picture of him that would not unnerve David. I explained simply that he had AIDS. David seemed calm and received the information with a nod. He explained that he knew of my research project and while he had never met anyone with AIDS, he was excited by the possibility of performing Francis's music in such an impressive setting. The relationship that was to grow between them during this short period was to have a lasting effect on David.

In recalling the rehearsal, I clearly remember the feelings of excitement and anticipation the three of us shared. During the first playing Francis sat with a look of steel. This unnerved David and myself to such an extent that the reading became extremely sloppy. Nevertheless, Francis was forgiving of our musical disarray and immediately concentrated on the details of interpretation. He became animated, considering various possibilities with enormous physical gestures that made me feel as if I was in a master class with an esteemed composer. David looked on open-mouthed, and soon began to share my understanding of how deeply important this time was for Francis. We concentrated on various sections, Francis directing the balance between instruments and overseeing phrasing and dynamics. After an hour of intense but constructive criticism the music began to speak.

The rehearsal bonded the three of us into a sense of unified purpose. Francis's remarks about David's style of playing and understanding of the score were at times harsh and over-critical, but David responded with complete respect. He took on board the many comments and tried repeatedly to adapt his playing to the interpretation Francis wanted. I was amazed to see a natural affinity growing between them. After Francis left we continued to practise. We knew this short time was important in refining his music for the performance the following week.

SESSION TWENTY-NINE – EMERGING PATTERNS

As he entered the room, Francis was obviously weaker:

> 'Thank you for the rehearsal. It was inspiring for me to hear my music played . . . I'm sleeping my life away at the moment . . . I'm going to play something.'

The improvisation opened with minor seconds based on D. These intervals formed the basis for the harmonic and melodic structure. The semitonal texture was balanced against quiet ethereal music in D major. The music unfolded from only a few themes. I experienced a range of feelings during his playing: passion, undefined anguish, and loss. It felt as if he was expressing something still more profound. I struggled with my perceptions as the music developed. Could it be that in music death was not frightening but beautiful and welcoming? Francis's expression revealed how deeply immersed he was in the developing improvisation. His music spoke of life and death simultaneously, as if he was tilting on an axis, viewing both sides of his being and reflecting where best to rest. His stream of communication was beautifully held and contained within an aesthetic form. The music attained a sense of knowing that for me epitomized the impermanence I had striven so long to understand.

I found myself reflecting on the fact that when he improvised he always appeared to be well and not affected by AIDS. Was it possible in music to cast aside the shackles of illness? Musical strengthening against physical deterioration is a major aspect of work with the dying. The cessation of physical symptoms in music, which often seems to be complete, can give a client release from pain and distress. I began to meditate on the profundity of musical expression Francis had attained. The balance in our relationship had now become all-embracing. Was it appropriate to allow myself to enter totally into his musical experience? When did I need to remain on the edge? It was usually possible from the opening notes of an improvisation to anticipate the level of intensity it would realize. I remember carrying out safety checks as the music progressed, allowing myself to withdraw if it became too intense for my own survival. Maintaining this balance was a constant struggle.

The improvisation continued for forty minutes. At the end there was the customary silence before he spoke:

'How did the music affect you? . . . You don't have to answer.'

I paused before speaking:

'I was caught under a musical spell.'
'What kind of things did you feel? What came to mind?'
'A sense of concentration, dichotomy, imbalance yet equilibrium.'
'A different kind of balance. All things are possible in music simultaneously . . . I felt very close in the music to how I was feeling, I was in touch with the way I was looking at things. To embrace a lot of . . . gosh, I'm tired . . . it did reflect . . . so . . . thank you . . . I felt that I was talking about what I was feeling now . . . what was going through me now. I wasn't digging up the past, I was connecting with the present. My own idiom has now emerged much more clearly. I couldn't tell you what that idiom is and yet I feel it just happens. My pattern is more clearly emerging. Having shed the acquired information, I'm now using that information. It's been reorganized in my own mind to represent my own feelings, which is a wonderful thing to happen . . . There's nothing more to say.'

He rose slowly and left the room. I remained alone.

126

WORLD AIDS DAY

The 1st of December and the service at Westminster Abbey came three days later. Francis had made no reference to the event at the end of the preceding session and I wondered what he might be thinking as the day approached. David and I had two more rehearsals, focusing on Francis's musical intentions. The more I reflected, the more significant I knew this occasion was for him and our relationship.

We arranged a further rehearsal in the Abbey on the afternoon of the performance to accustom ourselves to the very different acoustics. Walking down the central aisle I became totally engrossed in the grandeur of the building and the atmosphere that pervaded each section. It was difficult to imagine that in a few hours part of a music therapy session would be played here. My thoughts dwelt on the inspiration of the building and how well it matched Francis's struggles. It seemed utterly appropriate that his music was to live in the ambience of the beautiful architecture that soared around me. But the many practical responsibilities that had to be dealt with before David arrived for the rehearsal put an end to my transports of wonder. The rehearsal was far from satisfactory. There were difficulties in tuning, and the extensive echoes meant that our previous balancing of instrumental voices had to be drastically rethought. I had hoped that we would be able to record the complete service but the blurred resonance of the Abbey made this unrealistic.

Francis arrived an hour before the service. By this time I was anxiously pacing the changing room. I ushered him to a nearby chair and offered him refreshment, but he was far more interested in learning how the rehearsal had gone. I explained briefly the problems we had come across with the acoustics and recording. Convinced he would be distraught, I waited nervously for his response. To my relief he replied that he was not at all concerned that the service could not be recorded or that it might not be a perfect performance. He said that for him it was enough that it was happening and he was there. It did not strike me immediately as I was too caught up with my own fears, but Francis was absolutely serene. Through his extreme frailty he radiated a beauty that came from an inner sense of calm. Peacefulness replaced the distress he had been bringing to the sessions. As he sat waiting, I realized how far we had travelled. My nervousness disappeared. This man had battled and fought with his insecurities and pain, and had won. I wanted this performance to be a tribute to his courage and strength. He assured me again that he was not at all concerned that the performance would be perfect, he simply wanted us to play his music honestly. He took his leave to find his way to the front of the Abbey where he was to meet some friends. After accompanying him there, I returned to the changing room to wait for David.

By six-thirty everyone was seated. Francis sat by David and myself. The atmosphere was electric. The service consisted of prayers, readings and music. Francis's interlude came directly after a reading by Rabbi Lionel Blue. As David and I stood to take our places Francis smiled at us in a way that released our intense nervous energy. The playing soared. We became at one with his music and Francis became one with us. I do not remember anything of our playing other than that it flew. The audible silence that lingered after the music spoke of the collective experience of the whole congregation. Our months of suffering somehow seemed to lift. As the atmosphere returned to the present, Francis quietly rose and embraced David and myself.

I will never know the full extent of the impact this event had on David. He left soon after the service and discussed it with me only in passing the next time we met at the university. Francis's death was to have a much more powerful effect on him than I could ever have imagined. There appeared to be a bond between them that was private and unspoken. Their understanding of each other was separate and their own.

After the service Francis received great praise from his friends and members of the congregation. He looked the happiest I had ever seen him. The service was to act as the catalyst that would ultimately lead our intimately creative relationship outward to face the unknown ramifications of making his work accessible to a wider audience.

9

EXPRESSING THE DREAM FLOW – SESSIONS THIRTY TO THIRTY-THREE

And at the end I see: the great harmony is death.
To effect it, we must die. In life it has no place.
Paul Hindemith (1895–1963)
'Die Harmonie der Welt' (1957)

Exploring music and searching for the sources of musical intensity has preoccupied me for many years and has been fundamental to my growth as musician and music therapist. I began by examining music that spontaneously gripped and moved me. Then, by formulating methods of analysis and developing exercises, I attempted to identify the musical resources that captured the depth I felt was at the heart of communication in improvisation. The core elements I recognised were contained in a wide range of compositions that spanned much of musical history and ethnomusicology. One twentieth-century composition that exemplifies such musical surgence is the opera 'Oedipe' by Enesco. The combination of careful scoring, economical climaxes, exact vocal detail and carefully measured leitmotifs (Malcolm 1990) creates a score that is rich in emotion. This piece is an extended work of detailed tenderness and, in my opinion, could be used as an informative basis for study by music therapists. The musical world is full of such compositions waiting to be harvested in the quest to widen and enrich the improvisational resources of music therapy.

It was my intuition that aggression and pain could be expressed more powerfully by understatement and austerity than through extrovert musical gestures. This intensity of musical and therapeutic meaning, for which I had been searching all my life, I was now experiencing in Francis's improvisations. I felt he had reached a peak, a total sense of musical oneness. The description by Tweedie of how her teacher's singing affected her, also reflects my feelings about Francis's music at this time:

As soon as his voice filled the room it is as if I am transported to another place of being. The brain stops working. I do not listen with the mind. These songs of his, monotonous and in a language I do not understand, disturb something very deep within. It is like trying to get hold of long-forgotten memories; just glimpses, which are awakened by his voice and are somehow connected with him. It is as if I know the sound so well – as if it is a part of myself that I cannot understand. When I try to pin it down, it dissolves into nothing, just like the mist which disappears before it reaches you.

(Tweedie 1979, p. 32)

As I struggled to analyse Francis's expression, his music would simply disappear, metamorphosing into something totally new. His improvisations became completely part of me, shifting in and out of our momentary realities. Suspended sounds were caught, emerging into multi-layered portrayals of his inner world. His music reflected a sense of unity that was rapidly being denied him in his physical life.

SESSION THIRTY – LA FÊTE DES MORTS

Francis entered the room slowly, obviously in pain, and sat carefully at the piano:

'I've suddenly got three or four different ways of putting my hands on the piano . . . It's interesting.'

He began to improvise. A beautiful melody beckoned and drew me. Something deeply spiritual was being expressed and communicated. Every phrase spoke through the most sparing musical constructs. The improvisation became almost hymnal. There was beauty of sound and texture.

13 Audio Extract Thirteen – Session Thirty (5:34)
- **Opening music.**
- **Key: C minor.**

- **Simple chords that become momentarily louder.**
- **There is beauty and control. Chords with no melody.**
- **Francis introduces a musical toll that is used throughout to herald the end or beginning of a section:**

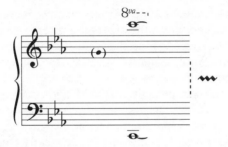

- **More melodic phrases emerge.**
- **A scale theme in sixths appears:**

- **This builds to a climax, before the C toll returns.**
- **The music becomes louder and more impassioned before slowly descending to a further toll and resting place.**

   (The improvisation continues for thirty-five minutes after the extract.)

It felt as if the music transcended its aesthetic quality in moving towards the essence of life itself. As the improvisation developed so the incorporeal quality of the music became ever more present. After a long pause the tempo accelerated. Images of flying and release emerged in a surging flood of immense energy. The tempo eased. As the improvisation drew to a close I contemplated the question that perhaps Francis was reaching towards the next stage on his journey? I was left with an impression that resonated with feelings of finality, balance and peace. As he turned to speak, his voice was almost a whisper:

'That was a drain on your resources I would imagine.'
'I have rarely heard such beautiful music.'
'I shall call that my funeral sonata. My requiem . . . *La fête des morts* . . .
It seemed to be a song of death which was remembering the continuity of life within the framework of dying. In a sense a broader picture. Amidst the dying there was living – there was a bittersweet awareness of that reality I think. They were contained within a general framework with the awareness that death is not all. It's a part of a living . . . I felt that somehow I was aware of expressing the dying though I was still aware of the content of life and the lyrical backcloth to the drama of

death. For me the improvisation was profoundly connected. There were different strands. Very much the expression of one. An expression of a richer tapestry that was beyond that which embraced a larger picture. What comes back into my mind is an early discussion at school about tragedy and comedy. What is included and what is left out to achieve different effects. Then there is the total approach. Laughter, tears, death and destruction. The focused way of dealing only with one specific aspect in excluding the others and heightening the immediate effect by exclusion. People like Homer and the early Greeks painted an entire picture of the human condition. Two different approaches. For me this was a broader . . . it required a certain balance of remembering what else there was in life. It seemed that, without upsetting the major picture that was one of death and departure, there were reminiscences and touches of colour. I was aware of the final open sound of accept-ance, almost an affirmation of the expression of saying "yes" to what is happening, to the meaning of life and death. Not noisy or overpower-ing, just that gentle expression of saying "yes". There was a fleeting moment I could have thrown all that away in a final section, which I rejected.'

'I'm glad you did. I don't think I could have taken any more.'

'No coda. I wanted to leave on that point, though I could have ex-pressed . . . revolt, I think, in using the single tone in a more violent and rejecting way. A violent display on the note G, of harsh repetition.'

He began to play repeated G's ( ). The tempo became faster,

moving away from the single tone towards a timbre that was complex and atonal. This short coda ended abruptly:

'Something like that. The feeling was there. I'm glad I was able to express that also. There was a very primitive feel about that. I think that it should be placed at the beginning and not at the end. It's like a short introductory tension which can then be followed by the main work. Somehow, it seems to put the delicacy of the opening chords into perspective. So this section would do very well as a prologue. I now see that this is an important part of my mental picture. It was there waiting. This music gives a background to the tranquillity again, it's the life and death dichotomy. The music balances the scenes of life and death.'

As he improvised, contemplating life and death together, I had the feeling that through his playing, which was now transcendent, his thoughts were actually being formed by music. Music itself had become an intuitive means of perception for him – a means that searched out indefinable realities, explored them, and simultaneously brought them to expression in the moment-by-moment flow of improvisation. His insights, which he then cognitively understood and could articulate so tenderly, were first realized through his freely open musical creativity. Truly, he had achieved an extraordinary inner oneness. I remember feeling apprehensive about the future yet exhilarated by the stage we had reached. This time was of critical importance for us both: for Francis in realizing his all-encompassing creative unity, and for me in absorbing these revelations of the powers inherent in musical creation.

SESSION THIRTY-ONE – FLIGHT

I found it difficult to tear my thoughts away from Francis during the week, my mind again and again returning to the unknown period of time we had left.

He began the next session by talking about his friend Tony:

'Last week's session was a requiem, due in part to the fact that my friend Tony was dying . . . He died that day . . . He moved into the lodge next-door to where I live. I thought I might play part of the improvisation at his funeral service . . . "All Saints Day", the triumph of life and death . . .'

I was stunned. He had never mentioned he had a friend who was ill with the virus. He obviously needed to talk about him:

. . . because I felt that there was something triumphal, it was about life and death. I thought the final coda I played should be at the beginning. When Tony died I had this primeval feeling of howling like a wolf. I was distressed and found this howl welling up inside. A very primitive feeling . . . I'm not sure if any of that came across in the final coda.'
'Yes, it certainly did!'
'Tony was someone I had befriended and supported. Then I realized that he had never asked for my friendship and had never asked for my support. I gradually withdrew when he had a crisis and nearly went berserk. I took such care of him, but he left in the middle of the night. I couldn't get through to him, and then he went into a rather neurotic high. It was clear that our values were different. What the awareness of death meant to him was to get in touch with what was really important to him and that was a showy car and money. That was the world he wanted to inhabit. I remember thinking, "What kind of civilization do we live in that gives a man such an impoverished sense of values?" I have this problem that I represent many of these values for people and I don't believe in them myself. I get foisted into representing other people's projections. Of course I couldn't substantiate any of those dreams of his. There was no reciprocity on the

basis of a present relationship because when he went off on this high of money and cars he didn't include me. The only time I got to see the car, I realized afterwards, was when he had run out of money for petrol. So he needed me to give him money so that I could have a drive. So gradually I withdrew. But I felt – I don't know why it touched some parental caring in me – that in a sense I had taken him under my wing as he was totally isolated. He touched a child-care feeling in me when he was dying. It affected me strongly even though I had not seen him for many months. The council, after two years, had finally found him a flat, but it was too late. I certainly had a reaction to his death. He died at the hospital on the day of our last session.'

He began to improvise. The music was harsh and violent, completely in opposition to the music of the previous session. It contained a tangible life-force that had been absent since our opening duets. The forcefulness soon diminished to a style that included inventions of intricate arpeggios alongside short melodic fragments. The music became more ethereal as the improvisation developed. At the end there was a dramatic silence:

'Very hard to express. I had a quite definite feeling of what I wanted to do . . . I'm not quite sure. It was an idea of shimmering sounds. I don't know why. Almost the expression of a sheer sense of beauty. To say disconnected from reality . . . I'm not sure it is. I think it must be related to something. I'm trying to express some kind of a dream . . . I wonder if it's . . . yes, a kind of dream flow. I don't know why . . . I felt it quite strongly. I wanted to create this picture.'
'I have no words.'
'It did say something to you?'
'Yes. But there are no words to describe it.'
'It's moved away from a more obvious labelling of angry, which I was. It's somehow transcended beyond, crossed over into something else. What I was trying to do on the piano – what exactly I felt I wanted to try and do – it was . . . in that sense . . . but I don't know why I should have wanted to express this today . . .

'It's not been a very positive week. A lot of death and my home-care hasn't come. Nobody is around, there are difficulties on all fronts. One could be tempted to fall into something that was escapist or puerile, but I loathe to agree to that. I don't think it's that very facile, it wasn't that . . . much more profound. A deeply rooted expression. It wasn't flight. It was flight in one sense, certainly perhaps *essor* in the French sense of the word, but it wasn't escape.'

He fixed his stare toward the window and spoke haltingly:

'I look forward to this hour. It's the whole week for me. It's what my whole life is about, in a sense of actually expressing myself, of being able to say more personally what's happening in my life.'

These times when Francis would so directly articulate the value and meaning music therapy held for him were very important for me. They reaffirmed the normally unspoken significance of our work. He continued:

'There was clearly an interaction during this improvisation. I was receptive and I didn't hesitate. I wanted to create this shimmering imagery of sound, which was almost creating a . . . an absolution. I respond to the fact that I do this right away. I have responded to you – you just open it up for me. I don't know what happens, because I don't do it anywhere else and I don't do it on my own. So there's very clearly a strong, creating, releasing interaction. But I think today it might, in a sense, have more coincidence of feeling rather than . . . certainly your mood was suited to mine. When you came in you were rather quiet and very serious. I felt immediately that I couldn't in any way engage in expression that was banal, or that the briefest of everyday occurrence would be permitted. It wasn't right somehow for the level of perception and feeling that we had attained. So in that way it was highly suited to the way I wanted to express myself. That of course can even extend to that, at a distance, one can influence people telepathically. The so-called theory of simultaneity. Apart from weaving these assumptions and ideas, the fact remains that one thing may be interlocked into something that is able to express to you and to me. You become at one with the music.'

His recognition that the relationship constituted the essence of our work was also important for us both. The relationship could be seen to be sacrosanct and, as he so rightly presumed, could not be recaptured outside. His appraisal made me realize how significant my demeanour was at the beginning of a session. It influenced the way he responded to me, which in turn affected the way he improvised. This confirmed that the human and musical content of our relationship permeated everything that happened in therapy. Even though I was not participating in the music-making, my influence on the course and continuance of the therapy process was in no way diminished.

SESSION THIRTY-TWO – SINGING

This session consisted mainly of conversation. At the beginning I could feel Francis's need to speak. His bearing communicated a sense of urgency:

'My life is now a continual – I don't want to use the word battle or struggle – but a continual effort. I attempt to express something though, to give expression to something which is transferable to a medium of expression. The tension between trying to express something and being

limited by the very concrete nature of the thing which you are trying to
achieve. How can you portray beauty and harmony and the sheer won-
drousness of things? How can you actually portray that? The answer is,
of course, people have tried and some have come close to achieving that
miracle.'
'I feel that perhaps you have.'
'Yes. I think gosh! I would have never believed a year ago that this was
possible. It was something that remained dormant and caused me dis-
satisfaction for a long time. That was the block, I think. That I was so
dissatisfied with the repetition of these very fixed, almost sacrosanct,
sacred bounds of written music. The Byzantine discussion of performance and technique. This really wasn't what I was about. I never felt
encouraged or supported in any attempt to be at one with the instrument. The whole teaching process is almost designed to remove any
perception of the unifying process . . . The totality of vision is destroyed
. . . That's inevitable, I suppose, as there are few people achieving that
feeling. How many teachers are even aware of it!'

As he continued, I felt as if he was attempting a recapitulation of our work:

'I have been moved in delight of myself – by what we have done together, because you made it possible. Some chemical magic, that I don't
feel the slightest hesitation in playing. I think you have a gift of saying
that life is good, and that what you do is good and is of infinite importance. It's a question of belief. You seem to spread the capacity to
believe. A very rare gift I think. Anyhow it's made my past journey all
possible.

'I sit here and think "How can I?" on one level – the level that I'm
amazed at the continuity, richness and absolute security of what I'm
doing. I'm not amazed at myself. It's a rather . . . it's so natural, so
automatic that it doesn't amaze me. I'm delighted by the validity. It
seems as though it is good and that it does convey expression. It does
convey meaning and certainly it speaks back to me – and I think it
speaks to you. So on one level I'm amazed it happens, but on another it's
naturally a part of me . . . It's what is behind this desire to give concrete
form to something. I suppose it really is an instinctive expansion of the
soul. It's almost as if we each have a song to sing. If you sing your song,
your life has meaning, but if that song is either destroyed or not allowed
to surface, then you are living very much a second-hand life. It was very
much the recovery of my song. I remember I said, "I don't know what to
sing? What is my song? Where is my song? I can't find it. Help me find it"
. . . I had seriously lacked the means of expression that was linked to my
own feeling and my own emotions – centred in my own creativity . . .'

He began to improvise.

14 Audio Extract Fourteen – Session Thirty-Two (4:45)
- **Opening music.**
- **Key: E flat major.**
- **An open simple melody with a tonic pedal provides a sense of security.**
- **A chordal scale theme is introduced.**
- **Descending and ascending chords.**
- **A pause creates a resting place, and is followed by harmonic clusters in the treble.**
- **The music moves forward for an instant before declining towards a return to the opening scale figures. The improvisation, however, is now more positive, with melodic material emerging.**
- **The music develops with structural simplicity.**
  (The improvisation continues for forty minutes after the extract.)

This music was truly Francis's song, a reflection of his soul released, with all exterior influences left behind. The improvisation was concentrated. A focus evolved that gently subsided towards the quiet reflective chords from which the music originally germinated:

> 'It's like a kind of limbo. Nowhere. Limbo is the old concept of not heaven and not hell, but where people used to go when they hadn't qualified for either.'
> 'Is that representative of how you are feeling?'
> 'I think it is – in the sense that I didn't have a very marked feeling before and I didn't have a lot of energy. That kind of state of suspension. What did you feel?'
> 'I thought it was finely tuned, quite extraordinary. It wasn't comfortable for me.'
> 'Disturbing?'

I struggled to find the word:

> 'I didn't find it disturbing exactly. More spiritually intense.'
> 'There wasn't any marked driving emotion. There was just something, somewhere else.'
> 'The opening was beautiful. Very uncluttered.'
> 'Yes, it does fit in with what I was saying before I played – about trying to express, give expression to some kind of beauty.'
> 'You achieved it there.'
> 'I was aware of being in a somewhat tenuous state. I felt that I . . . almost as if it were floating without any visible means of support.'
> 'The pedal was very grounding.'
> 'The first passage, like the organ note, was anchoring. It was reminis-

137

cent of different themes, of holding on to something. It was a rooting experience.'

'I'm amazed how you use the minimum of notes to express yourself.'

'I see that, listening back, and I feel it myself, the reduction and simplicity – complex simplicity. It's a sort of sparseness, but then it's not empty – there's nothing in excess. The words are so difficult to find. It's dreadful trying to express through the verbal form. Certainly it's become very finely balanced. There is an economy, it says very directly and very straightforwardly what I want to say without any dressing-up, hesitation or repetition. I'm actually finding my own form of expression – I do believe that it must be true. This is the value of a cultural tradition, and why it is so important that tradition should be available to everyone. That is what feeds the soul. You must first take in and absorb our heritage, the sum of human heritage in different ways. Out of that emerges your own voice. But you have to use the instruments that your ancestors have left you. You may, of course, move on to create new ones, but essentially I think you get the benefit of the great wealth of exploration and experience of your fellow human beings. Then you shed the pastiche. Initially you find a lot conjuring up out of what you have learnt. If you are prepared to work through that and get in touch with your own self and trust yourself – as I have learnt to do with you – then that just slips into the background and becomes the elements. Then you assemble those elements on your own. It's almost as if you use bricks but you don't use the façade. Like so often they take out the inside of a building and leave the façade. I find that it's not something which I like. If you have a building which is worth preserving, you should preserve it, very much in the way it was originally calculated, because the whole thing is a part of the whole. Just to keep a façade and walk in and find it's got nothing to do with the exterior at all is futile. So, in that sense, one no longer has big blocks of things – past musical influences. You have just individual bricks and they are shed more and more. That's the difference between Czerny and Beethoven. It can be technically brilliant but it can have nothing to say, nothing at all. Beethoven was trying to break the bounds and striving to escape from the chains. He had a living world within his soul.'

Through a process of recognizing earlier influences, acknowledging their value, then passing through and beyond them, Francis had discovered an expression that was the true essence of musical self. Now, it was as if in this solo landscape he was finding the summarizing balance necessary to his continuing life and impending death.

SESSION THIRTY-THREE – INVOCATION OF LIFE

I was unaware at the time that this was our final session. Francis seemed tired. He sat silently at the piano and began to play.

15 **Audio Extract Fifteen – Session Thirty-Three (7:26)**
(Forty minutes after the opening. Last two sections of the improvisation)
– Tonal centre: C minor.
– Dense chromatic clusters evolve towards a melodic theme:

– **This is curtailed with rhythmic stabbing that becomes gradually slower.**
– **Syncopated figures produce a sense of being unsettled. There is nothing to hold on to. A macabre musical portrait?**
– **A section of octaves develop toward extrovert chromaticism.**
– **The music eventually rests in E major followed by an impassioned section that hints back to the C minor of the opening.**
– **A long pause creates a resting place.**
– **Repeated G's in octaves gradually diminish to a single G that becomes slower and fainter, dying away to nothing.**
– **End of improvisation.**

What was he trying to express? Where was this energy coming from? The music was so dramatically different from that of the previous sessions. The pause before the final octave section was agonizing. The sound died away, tone by tone, to a single tone. Then nothing. The ensuing silence seemed like a lifetime's extension of the music. It bored into my soul, shredding my emotions. How much closer to the edge could Francis get? I was afraid to be a part of these glimpses into what felt like the other reality of death. Was it possible to experience this otherworld ascent and remain in the world of the living? I consciously steadied myself in preparation for his words:

'Yes . . . It's so magical . . . I sit down and play that. It really puts other things into perspective.'
'For me too.'
'It revises my sense of values and feelings. It makes me more secure in my leave of life. It reminds me of an ability of the soul . . . Thank you for being there. I would like to name this improvisation "For Colin." '

'Thank you for sharing.'

'I think music has an overall power that is greater than the other art forms. It seems to me that it embraces the entire sphere of expression, and I think is able to include and encompass so much. It goes beyond the poetic and dramatic use of words, beyond the power of painting or the shock and impact of architecture. These things happen as well, but somehow music lifts everything on to a different plane of totality. I suppose that might be because one's expression in music is essentially different. Mind and soul are opened up by music. I have this image of a sphere, and different forms of expression – in that somehow, music enfolds and encompasses the entire ball, lifting it to a different height. I felt I was expressing only what I was totally in contrast with. Feeling without fireworks or padding. It expressed the purity. A bitter-sweet invocation of the transitory nature of life. The touch of – not anger – of bitter-sweet, that life comes to an end. It's something you have to grasp as it goes past. I think there's that unique human feeling of death that has been developed with such poignancy. The poignancy of the human condition is that we don't, for the most part, accept. We ask why. We say: "Why should there be so much pain and so much joy?" In the end you move out, that's been your life-span. It is the awareness of the ephemeral nature of life, which I have often suspected not everyone has. I think perhaps many human beings keep themselves closer to the animal feeling in the sense that they don't want to think about death. They are either convinced that everything is lasting or they convince themselves that an awareness of death is not necessary. So, I think, for many people, it is the way they choose to live. People who have a perception or artistic feeling are striving to express and capture one form or another. The awareness of the eternal that lies behind the temporary or transient, and the constant living in nostalgia. Nostalgia for the past, for the future and very often for the present. It's not often that we really live the moment. I think in this improvisation we were expressing the moment . . . I am so glad to be able to get here. It was a struggle.'

This was the last music Francis played before he died. After the session, I was unaware of its feeling of closure. I simply felt a great sense of relief at all he had attained and how much he had brought together; his air of peace and fulfilment stayed with me. Sitting outside the music therapy room later in the day with Leslie, the reflexologist, our conversation turned to Francis. She thought he looked extremely ill and somehow distant, and expressed her view that he might be too ill to make the journey to Lighthouse again. What was it about his demeanour that betrayed this sense of ending that she so clearly saw? Why had not I seen it? Looking back at the session, I then felt the finality of his music. I left Lighthouse feeling heavy in spirit and tired.

10

AFTER THERAPY – A FINAL
DANCE OF CREATION

Here is no final grieving, but an abiding hope.
The moving waters renew the earth.
It is spring.

Michael Tippett (1905–)
'A Child of our Time'

I arrived at Lighthouse for the next session to find a note waiting at reception
asking me to phone the Middlesex Hospital in London. I was informed that
Francis had been admitted the previous evening for observation and that his
condition was stable. He had left a message that he would like to see me later
that day if at all possible. When I arrived, he was sitting up in bed, his
penetrating eyes conveying urgency and life. He explained that he had suddenly lost the use of his legs and had been informed by the consultant that
morning that it was unlikely he would regain their use. He spoke with a sense
of detachment, as if his symptoms belonged to someone else. The hidden
concern beneath this dialogue was 'What is going to happen to our music
therapy relationship?' Shock disabled me from raising the issue we both knew
would have to be discussed before I left. It was Francis who broached the subject, saying clearly and dispassionately that it would now be impossible for
him to attend Lighthouse for sessions and to continue our music therapy relationship in the form it had taken until now. My thoughts were: 'How can he
be so clinical? Is this really the end? Surely he might get better? Our work is
too important for it to stop now.'

He explained that he had had time to consider the options for our relationship, but that whatever was decided it should be discussed jointly. He saw that
we had three alternatives. First, to discontinue our relationship completely;
second, to try to re-establish our music therapy roles in different venues; or
third, to become friends instead of therapist and client. He paused and asked
me for my feelings. There was no question as to which option I favoured, I
had come too far with this man to abandon him now. I knew too the option
he would favour, and that deep down he must be sure of my response. I told
him I wanted us to become friends. There was a long silence as we began to

adjust to a new way of being together and responding to each other. The thought of friendship was liberating yet forbidding. Was it ethically correct to do this? I had certainly never before heard of such a change in a therapeutic relationship. Ultimately, I had only my feelings to follow and I knew without question this was the right course for us both.

We stayed together for many hours that afternoon, not always alone, as visitors and nurses passed through the ward. Gradually we adjusted to a new way of existing. We talked little about our decision and what the consequences would be. It was enough to know that the situation had changed: we had begun again. Towards the end of my visit Francis told me of his decision to stay with friends in Milton Keynes if his health continued to deteriorate. Should this happen, he had decided to leave all the trappings of his life in London behind, including all his friends. He did not want to die in London. He stared at me intently as he explained that one of the few people he wanted to continue seeing was me.

I found it impossible to express the feelings aroused by his decision. I knew the uniqueness of our relationship, though plumbing its full depths began in earnest with the writing of this book, and I believe will never cease. But as our relationship moved into the limits imposed by his illness, I realized that our role as friends would bring its own challenges.

Endings form the essence of life itself:

> The fragility and delicate balance when working with endings is an integral part of all our work. By beginning we have to face endings. How do we help our clients face endings, and how do we face them ourselves? The ending of an improvisation can often point to the efficacy of the therapeutic process during the interaction, or at the moment of contact or in future development. Trusting endings is one of the most difficult but pertinent aspects of our work.
>
> (Lee 1991, p. 4)

Death bestows a reality that is uneasy, seeming to undermine the reason for life itself. Rinpoche (1992, p. 16) suggests that: 'Perhaps the deepest reason we are afraid of death is because we do not know who we are.' My fear and denial of the finality of Francis's death seemed an impenetrable abyss of emotions. He was the first person to need my presence on this fundamental level during the dying process, and I would have to call on whatever understanding of death and dying I had gained in order to help him traverse this final chapter of his life. Although I felt unprepared and nervous, I had to be resolute.

He decided to move to Milton Keynes soon after his hospitalization. It was now a few days before Christmas and, preparing to spend part of the holidays with my parents in the Midlands, I arranged to visit him on Boxing Day. He asked me to bring the recording of his final session. As I drove to meet him conflicting emotions moved within me: the situation seemed unorthodox yet natural, confusing yet logical. Allowing my thoughts to flow freely, I began to understand for the first time since our final session the rightful balance of our new relationship. To raise worrying ethical interpretations was inappropriate. With this realization came a sense of inner calm and peacefulness. I became aware of the need to let Francis know how much he had given me through our work.

When I arrived he was still in bed. As I waited, getting to know his friends, I wondered how physically changed he might be. He was eventually carried downstairs and I saw, to my dismay, that he had changed beyond all recognition. He was skeletal. On being placed in the armchair he began to cry uncontrollably, a weeping of intense, unremitting pain. It felt like a howl of the final denunciation of life. I did not want to see him like this; I could not bear to see him suffering. Our relationship was built on respect, on the perception that he was always strong and dignified, and I struggled desperately to see beyond his decline, to allow our souls to meet as they had done so many times before in music. After a long shared stillness, during which he continued to weep quietly, he asked to listen to the improvisation from his final session. I expressed my feeling that I was unsure if this was a good idea, for him or myself. He quietly but firmly reiterated his request, and I realized how great his need to hear the music was. As the music began I felt a lifting of his spirit, as if he was now home. It was borne in me that he had been waiting for this moment since the final session itself, wanting the remembrance of how he had lived in music. He relaxed completely as he closed his eyes and became at one with his creativity. By the end of the recording his friends had left the room.

For a long time we sat in silence, unable to speak and break the spell. When he did, his voice was hushed and restrained. He asked that I record his final words about our work:

'This time had been one of wonderment and discovery for me. I have journeyed to the farthest reaches of my soul and expressed that sense of freedom we all have but seldom have the opportunity to express. Music therapy has allowed me to explore a sense of innate hostility that I ultimately needed to acknowledge in coming to terms with my death. Through improvisation the beauty of my being was allowed to surface through a final dance of creation.'

Again, the silence that followed gave our relationship a depth beyond understanding. I waited to find the space to speak, to explain that I would try and visit him as much as I could from London during the coming weeks. We discussed the fact that his time was limited and that however our relationship developed, it would be within the constraints of his inevitable physical weakening. He told me of his decision not to have a funeral. While I was shocked at first by this disclosure, I saw upon reflection the importance to him of not having a normal passage after his death. He was estranged from his family and had said most of his goodbyes before leaving London. His life had certainly not been conventional, so why should his departure from it be different? I wondered how this decision would affect those left behind. When all the practical aspects had been discussed, I paused, then asked him if I could speak. My monologue, that I had gone over so many times in the car, felt clumsy and unfocused. He regarded me with an understanding that made me realize it was unimportant what I said, rather that it needed to be said, alone and for him. I relaxed. As I acknowledged my love for him and all that he had given me, a unity arose between us. I saw that it had been immaterial that we had met in the context of AIDS, and that we had taken the roles of therapist and client. What had been the most important reality in our relationship was that we had been two equal individuals sharing so profoundly in music.

As I prepared to leave, it was with a feeling of reluctance, for there was still so much for us to share. We knew that there could be no guarantee of any future time together and that each goodbye could be the last. On leaving, I impressed upon his friends that if he needed me I would come. Within two days of my visit I received a phone call to say that he appeared to be dying and that he had asked to see me. I bundled together some clothes and drove to their house, arriving during the early hours of the morning.

By the time I arrived, Francis's condition had improved and he was able to sit up in bed and converse quite easily. I spent the whole day sitting at the foot of his bed, simply talking. We filled in the gaps of our personal lives, and discussed the trivial aspects of existence as well as the most serious and significant. We laughed, scorned our colleagues and relatives, and solved the enigmas of life. There was a lightness about him I had not experienced before, as if his travelling was over and he could now spend time relaxing from passion and searching. Toward the end of the day the tone of the conversation became more serious as he asked that we discuss what would happen to his recordings after his death. Apart from my research, which he had seen at various stages of its development, he thought we should consider the possibility of making his words and music available to a wider audience. One particular matter that was preoccupying his thoughts was that his improvisations should be seen as works of art, besides retaining their therapeutic origins. It was not that he wanted to deny their source, but rather that the music might help other people travelling similar routes, and inspire musicians concerning the aesthetics of music therapy. After much deliberation, because I had not previously considered the possibility of publishing our work, we agreed there was enough material on which to base an extended case-study. I promised him that after his death I would begin the preparation of a manuscript. My pledge comes to fruition in the completion and publication of this book.

This day together was special for us both, and I look back on it when I think of our ending. Our relationship found the balance that was right for its natural conclusion. Three days later Francis was moved to a local hospice. His condition had weakened to the stage where his friends were no longer able to provide the care he needed. I visited as soon as I could. Entering his room a sudden rush of panic overcame me. I had been too busy with the logistics of getting there to think what might happen when I arrived or how ill he might be. Standing by his bedside I gazed down at this shadow of a man so clearly on the brink of life and death. He smiled, gently moving his lips as if to speak. I sat by his side and took his hand: 'Thank you for coming,' he whispered. His physical presence was slowly fading. 'It's difficult for me to talk. Can we share in silence?' 'Of course,' I replied. For the rest of the time we sat without speaking. He occasionally requested, by a nod, that I moisten his dry lips with a damp cloth. There was a mutual understanding that had now gone beyond words. Leaving the hospice that afternoon a deep sense of peace came over me as I accepted that it was unlikely that we would ever meet again. He died two days later.

Recalling my feelings, I was unprepared for the despair that seized me on the day Francis died. Arriving back at my flat, my first thought was that I needed isolation in which to say my final goodbye. But the reality changed, the repose I thought we had captured during our last time together suddenly turned to blackness and confusion. I wanted to be alone yet did not know how to grapple with my feelings of hopelessness and loss. Francis had at last been released, yet I could not fully believe our time together was over. Randomly selecting a recording of one of his improvisations I sat in the corner of my lounge and listened. The extraordinary thing was I do not think I heard the music at all. This was a final letting go, over which there was no control. It was the beginning of my bereavement.

I knew I had to inform David, the young clarinettist who had played at the service on World AIDS Day. I realized that he would be unaware of what had happened during the Christmas vacation, so on the first day back at the university I made a point of finding him to explain Francis's sudden deterioration and subsequent death. As I did, I was reminded of the bond that had grown so naturally between them, for David was totally shocked. This was the first person he had known who had died. Later in the year he wrote a song that he performed both at a student review and in a lunch-time concert at Lighthouse:

> Hey, a friend is gone.
> As I wipe away the tears,
> I can still feel you strong.
> I imagined man was immortal,
> That no-one could ever die.
> But now illusions are shattered,
> And I'm left to wonder why.
> I know that I shouldn't grieve.
> In time it comes to everyone.
> But in hope I breathe,
> Because I don't believe you're gone.

145

Francis died as I was co-organizing a conference on music in palliative care entitled 'Music for Life.' We had planned to present a paper jointly, giving a summary of our sessions, the first time the work was to appear in the public arena. We had discussed the conference some months earlier and agreed it would be exciting to co-present, sharing music therapy with the audience from the perspectives of both client and therapist. As Francis became weaker we realized this would be impossible. I changed the programme accordingly and decided that I would play extracts from sessions, read Francis's words and intersperse them with my own personal thoughts and evaluations.

The day of the conference came a month after his death. The awareness that there would be no funeral had begun to penetrate more deeply, leaving me bereft and unsettled. There had not been, nor would there be, any formal closure, no container in which to place my grief. Superficially, it seemed that Francis had not considered the feelings of those close to him. 'How could he have denied me the necessary context in which to say farewell?' I asked myself, despite the knowledge that he had given me every opportunity in our final hours to work through our mutual endings. As the conference drew nearer I knew it would have major implications for me in setting to rest my emotions.

It is difficult to describe my feelings about the day without resorting to sentimental descriptions of the presentation and how I reacted during and after the paper. There was a sense, as I stood to begin, that I would not be able to find the calmness to hear Francis's music, read his words and speak freely about my feelings. The hour travelled at lightning speed. It was as if someone had taken control and I was watching from afar, speaking and commenting on things that were in some way unconnected to me. The silence after his final improvisation brought with it a profundity that seemed to pervade the whole audience. I could hardly bear to share it – I felt it was strangling me. There was an almost intolerable suspension of time, until eventually I was released from the conference hall to a space where I could be alone. For the first time since Francis's death I wept.

Some months later a memorial service was held in his local church. While his friends had respected his wish not to have a formal funeral they felt an overriding need to say their goodbyes in a formalized setting. The service felt strange as I did not know many of the people present. Looking at the faces I wondered what relationships they had had with Francis. Did any of them know of our work? I improvised a small reflective piece intended to be an expressive confirmation of our relationship. I am not sure why, but I felt, then as now, strangely isolated from the whole proceedings. Returning for tea at the vicarage where he had lived brought further personal confusion. He had stayed here and yet I did not feel his presence. As I prepared to leave, the vicar, his friend and landlord, asked if I would like to see his room. I agreed with enormous apprehension. This was a difficult, although purging, time; my feelings are too personal to be included here. Francis had asked that I be given all his music plus an essay he had written on the arts, creativity and life. This essay appears as a coda to this book; I hope it adds a vivifying dimension to his voice.

Since the time of Francis's death I have completed two major pieces of writing: my PhD Dissertation (Lee 1992) and a co-edited book on art therapy and music therapy research (Gilroy and Lee, eds, 1995). These projects unavoidably delayed the preparation of this book, but I can now see the benefit of allowing time to elapse before beginning the portrayal of the work we did. Life, death and dying, beginnings and endings, take the form of continuous life-cycles. Whatever these events, they contain the essential elements of birth, growth and death. Through Francis's death I began to understand the power of bereavement. Writing this book has been an illuminating and tender process, rekindling the failures and successes of what must be seen as a unique music therapy journey. Perhaps, as I begin to put the final touches to this description of our time, I will be able to say goodbye to this chapter of my life. My relationship with Francis continues.

11

AFTERWORD

>. . .If architecture is frozen music
>then creativity is the supreme musical experience,
>the song of songs which irrefragably state
>the divine totality and ever present eternal life.
>(Francis, 'Coda', this volume)

My original intention was to leave this book open-ended, concluding with the description of Francis's death. But during the writing I came to see the need for a final chapter that would consider the impact of our work on perceptions of music and the therapeutic process. I hope this additional text will facilitate questions which will contribute to a deeper understanding of the role of music with people who are dying. The final summation of my experiences is intended to offer support to music therapists who work with people with HIV and AIDS. Additionally, I hope to encourage people living with the virus to consider the possibilities that music therapy offers for exploration, expression and growth. Francis's voice is heard again in a coda to this chapter as he puts forward his views on human talents, human needs, and the arts.

QUESTIONS AND PROCESS

One of my greatest concerns is that the reader might too quickly draw conclusions from the work that Francis and I did. It was a vital discovery in my research that answers are intrinsically less important than questions: questions themselves are enlightening; questions hold the key to a greater understanding of music therapy. My research gained clarity through searching, rather than by empirical analysis. Answers did emerge at various points, but these moments were always unexpected. I learned not to be always seeking conclusions, but to live with the openness of not knowing. Just as our existence is a constant evolution of challenges, so new perspectives in music therapy mean that practice can never be constant or fully known. Coming to firm conclusions is rather like setting in stone assumptions about a creativity that is as fragile and ever-changing as the mist. If in any way I have been able to present Francis's musical and verbal testament without making his ideas sacrosanct then I will have treated his legacy with the respect it warrants.

In the opening chapter I explained that psychological or psychotherapeutic interpretations would not be incorporated in this book. At first sight, this may have seemed a bold step as music therapists constantly try, through assessment, to understand the process of their work. This natural probing is at the heart of the development of music therapy, and without it the profession would surely stagnate. Do the boundaries of description in this book then limit my ability to convey the complex dynamics in my relationship with Francis? I have also expressed my wish that other music therapists consider the connections between that relationship and their own approach or theoretical orientation. By leaving the book at a descriptive level, do I put readers in danger of misunderstanding the complex issues of music and the therapeutic alliance? A psychotherapeutic interpretation could perhaps have added a richness, similar to that in an allied arts therapy single case-study text (Dalley, Rifkind and Terry 1993) in which the descriptions from client and therapist are placed within a theoretical framework. However, having lived intensely in all the dimensions of Francis's unique music therapy journey I resolved to present it without interpretation or in-depth analysis. There is, I believe, intrinsic richness in documenting the therapeutic process, comprehensively, unambiguously and without appraisal. Francis himself rejected analysing his experiences, and my argument is similar: detailed assessment can at times detract from the essence of the phenomena one is striving to understand. Music therapy is validated on its own terms; to assume that it needs to look to more established models to clarify its practice means there is danger of diluting, even adulterating its inherent processes in order that it may be understood in the accepted terms of another discipline. The true essence of music and the therapeutic relationship surely lie within the ethereal qualities of their own form rather than within the more concrete elements of other theoretical orientations.

A further component of the book are my subjective evaluations. The decision I took to be personally and professionally honest was difficult. Music therapy writings, outside the bounds of countertransference, rarely discuss the feelings of the therapist. There is a danger therefore of the therapist 'knowing best', of the process being guided from the therapist's knowledge and expertise. With Francis this was certainly not the case. He was never passive: he made it clear from the outset that the shaping of the therapeutic process was equally his. While he acknowledged the roles of therapist and client, he accurately surmised that in music these boundaries became unimportant: music itself held the key to an essential understanding of his experience, and it was on music that our relationship was unequivocally based. The danger I foresaw in describing my feelings was that they might reduce the value of our relationship, that honesty might slide into sentimentality. Throughout the process of writing, my thoughts were concerned with the boundaries of self-disclosure. I could so easily have allowed the book to become a description of how we 'searched for the Holy Grail.' In my initial sketches there was indeed a sense of trying to attain the unattainable. With each draft of the manuscript I carefully re-examined the subjective elements, seeking to balance appraisal with the spirit of the therapeutic process.

So what does this book have to offer professionals and potential clients? Being a single case-study means that the reader has access to all the stages of a complete therapeutic process. The unabridged description of a music therapy journey gains in depth of communication through audio musical examples, integral to the text. The client is uniquely present in his improvisations: his statements are heard in his music as in his transcribed verbal explorations.

THE PARADOX OF MUSIC

Improvisation is at the heart of this book. In Chapter 2 I review some of the few evaluations available of the use of improvisation in palliative care. The literature considers improvisation among a variety of clinical approaches. These include song-writing, listening, guided imagery and verbal communication (Munro 1994). At this stage in the development of the field, there are relatively few examples in which improvisation is incorporated as the main therapeutic medium (Aldridge and Neugebauer 1990, Delmonte 1995, Lee 1995). Without doubt, in the face of death and dying, improvisation that requires activity from both client and therapist should be handled with extreme care, but as in the case of John in Chapter 2 (see p. 23) improvisation offers unique expressive and communicative channels, even though a client may be outwardly weak. Here the situation demanded improvisation, even though John's physical situation might have initially suggested improvisation to be inappropriate, but his insistence on coming to music therapy and his determined use of the instruments unquestionably pointed to the need for live, responsive, interactive music. Even though the therapeutic process is not always so clearly initiated, John's example demonstrates that with sensitive and resourceful handling, improvisation can play a vital role throughout the many levels of dying.

Bruscia, in his book on improvisational models of music therapy (1987), differentiates between the use of music *as* therapy (music providing the main medium for the therapeutic process) and *in* therapy (music providing a medium secondary to other therapeutic models). He further explains that many approaches use a combination of both, either individually or collectively. Francis would have placed his work firmly in the first category: music *as* therapy. Even though his verbal reflections were substantial, they served to elucidate, not diminish the power of his musical experiences. The investigation of one single improvisation in Chapter 4, and my unpublished research (Lee 1992), exemplifies my belief that detailed qualitative inquiry can highlight the essential foundations and components of music *as* therapy.

150

Bunt (1994) states that: 'Music and music-making can be a focus of real beauty and transformation, helping us to define our humanity and all that is vibrant in living to our creative potential' (p. 187). The paradox of music is that while it has the potential to transform our sense of beauty, it is intrinsically man-made, yet a life-giving force. It is this dichotomy that places it so essentially within the realms of the dying. While music can help define our living, can it by virtue of its nature allow a sense of our dying? For Francis, music was a therapeutic means of lucidly reviewing his life working through to the inevitable transformation of death. His musical expressions were multi-layered and profound: there was constant electricity and an ever-present sense of the unknown.

If we look at the harmonic framework of sessions (Figure 5: core harmonic centres) it is possible to consider questions that relate musical expression to therapeutic outcome. The implied tonal direction shows a circular move throughout the sessions from C major to C minor. The commentary on session fourteen, Chapter 6, concentrates on the balance between major and minor, which I suggest parallels the therapeutic difference between security and insecurity. It is further implied that Francis used this polarity to express ambiguity. What does this tell us about the music therapy process as a whole? Does it confirm Cooke's view (1959) that major expresses pleasure and minor sadness? I think that would be an oversimplification. Francis was keenly aware of the importance of harmonic cores and modulations. In terms of therapeutic effect, the harmonic basis was essential in matching his emotional state. It was clear to me that he considered precisely: a) the foundation of his harmonic language, b) the overall infrastructure of developmental modulations, and c) the relationship between harmonic core and the tonal centre with which each improvisation began and ended. Each expressive venture was independent yet part of the whole. The use of major and minor reflected his slow physical deterioration. There were times when he would exhibit clear signs that his life was fading, only to contradict these impressions by bursts of well-being. His decline never followed a consistent pattern. His development of harmonic openness and uncertainty were to me clear manifestations of the uncertain nature of his illness, frustration with which was often the reason for his confrontational nature, and for my insecurity as therapist. Francis described a sense of leaving a door open, allowing his expression only to be glimpsed at. He said: 'As soon as you've caught it, it shies away.' I believe that there was a spiritual connection between the move from major to minor and his struggles between life and death.

ON BEING A MUSICIAN AS CLIENT IN MUSIC THERAPY

Music therapy with musicians is sparsely documented (Erdonmez 1993, Lee 1995, Priestley 1994, Scheiby 1991). The work available addresses the therapeutic process but not the specific considerations of working with musically

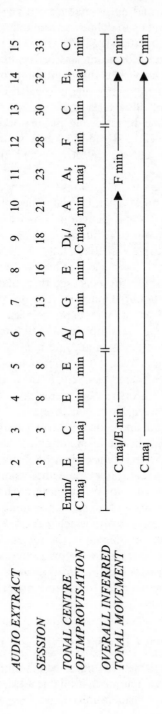

AUDIO EXTRACT	1	2	3	4	5	6	7	8	9	10	11	12	13	14	15
SESSION	1	3	3	8	8	9	13	16	18	21	23	28	30	32	33
TONAL CENTRE OF IMPROVISATION	Emin/ C maj	E min	C maj	E min	E min	A/ D	G min	E min	Db/ C maj	A min	Ab maj	F min	C min	Eb maj	C min

OVERALL INFERRED TONAL MOVEMENT

C maj/E min ——————▶ F min ——————▶ C min

C maj ————————————————————————▶ C min

Figure 5   Core Harmonic Centres

articulate clients. I would like to consider some of the questions that have arisen and the consequences these have had for my subsequent work with other musicians, all of differing abilities.

Francis's musicianship gave the therapeutic process a potentiating level of musical immediacy. After his initial musical disclosure he spent the first half of our sessions shedding his past to attain a sense of his latent musical self. The second stage was more complex and yielded two insights:

1 One might believe that musicians in therapy would find difficulty in breaking free from pre-ordained musical thought. At times, this is the case. But more often than not, once the possibilities of freedom from theoretical constraints are explained – as they were with Francis – musicians find no difficulty in exploring improvisation. Initially improvising at a superficial level, they are usually able to move on to express their feelings directly and finely.

2 A related and more significant perspective is that relinquishing influences from established composers and styles can have the effect of allowing the intricacies of the therapeutic process to surface. Stepping beyond established conventions of rhythm, melody, harmony and structure is often the necessary step towards finding the musical freedom that allows true therapeutic growth. From this dissolution a new sense of expressive form may emerge. Once this has been achieved, past musical concerns often return to serve the direction of the music, rather than dominate it. The contradiction is that on one level it is not difficult to invite musicians to improvise, while on another, it is often more difficult for such clients to express their inner musical lives.

Being a musician as client, and working with a musician as therapist, are both liberating experiences. Musicians often lose spontaneity in their trained renderings of other people's music: improvisation permits the intuitive expression of a musician's authentic sense of musical self. For the therapist there is often real testing of musical ability. Francis reminded me that my musical proficiency was important: ' . . . the expertise of your musical input is vital. I expect your musical inventions to be of the highest order, otherwise I would not have been prepared to travel personally.' The therapist must therefore be assured of his or her improvisational skills when working with musicians. This does not mean that the music therapist has to be up to virtuoso standard. It is possible to work with musicians who have superior musical skills; what is important is to listen carefully to their musical contribution. It is not enough to think in terms of an overall musical structure. The therapist must consider the smallest intricacies of expression within the musical relationship.

For the musician-client there can be the experience of real meeting, both in creative music-making and the developing relationship with the therapist. Perhaps this is reason enough for musicians to enter music therapy. Every form of therapy requires that the client should have a presenting problem, and music therapy, at present, is no exception. Francis would never have considered music therapy had it not been for his AIDS diagnosis, but while the reason for his referral always remained the musical dialogue ultimately developed into something beyond his physical condition – something greater than the human condition altogether.

MUSIC AND WORDS

My struggle to find an equilibrium between music and words that would provide an appropriate therapeutic dialogue was constantly challenging, and formed a large part of my supervision in counselling. Because my beliefs about the potency of music therapy were firmly rooted within the musical experience, I resisted the idea of verbal explorations being of equal importance. What Francis highlighted however was that if words came directly from music they could be equally meaningful. It was rare for him to predict a direction for his music before improvising, but verbal descriptions after the improvisations afforded him opportunities to validate and clarify his experience. I came to realize that he needed to articulate in words and music with similar precision. As the therapeutic process deepened, his use of words changed: they became less structured and more flowing. From session twenty-seven onwards, there were more pauses and rests. He seemed less clear about what he wanted to say. As he faced the unknown, his thoughts became more searching and his statements enigmatic. He finally relinquished his verbal searches as words became redundant in expressing the essence of his musical living.

Francis's statements fall into two categories: a) the times when he would discuss the wider implications of his life and b) direct explorations of musical experience. On the one hand, he talked about his perceived lack of recognition and his sense of being abandoned by those around him – I always had the impression that he felt alone and misunderstood. On the other hand he would discuss the ephemeral qualities of improvisation and the mystery of the therapeutic process. The final sessions contained verbal searches of great insight. He discussed music with deftness and clarity. The appraisal of session eight (p. 55) reveals his understanding of musical processes. He spoke of music in its several roles: in itself, in the therapeutic process, and as a medium for rendering conscious thought into subjective understanding. He considered intervals, downward phrases and how the combinations of a small group of notes in the generative cell were important in translating his feelings. It is interesting that session thirty-two, the penultimate session, consisted mainly of discussion. Perhaps he wanted to complete his verbal legacy with a final summary of his work? I remember clearly his comments on my role as therapist and the connections he made between singing and life.

Can words address the complex issues of death and dying with the same potency as music? Francis rarely spoke in depth of his fear of death, and what he did say sounded like an afterthought. In session twenty (p. 107) he said: 'I'm trying to get myself ready for death in that I'm imposing a pattern on myself. I can die angry, why shouldn't I die angry? I don't have to die at peace.' Later, in session thirty (p. 130): '. . . the awareness that death is not all. It's a part of a living process. I felt somehow I was aware of expressing the dying, though I was still aware of the content of life and the lyrical backcloth to the drama of death.' Comments such as these were both poignant and resolute. That life and death are inextricably linked seemed to be at the core of his expression, verbally and musically. The assumption that we die as we live was highlighted in his recognition that he was fully prepared to die angry. I was relieved that often he did not require a response at these times. In contrast, his musical representations of endings were developed and clear, as can be heard in audio extract ten from session twenty-one (p. 110). That this improvisation continued at the same level of intensity for almost fifty minutes gives us some indication of the power music had to transcend the pain and despair he experienced as his physical life began to slip away. The improvisations that follow all contain a directness of musical thought that, while every listener may interpret them differently, I believe express the essence of a dying man. Words could not have expressed his most inward feelings with the same magnitude as his improvisations.

Nevertheless, words indisputably have an important role in music therapy. In some approaches their use is central to the therapeutic process (Priestley 1994) while with others they are secondary to the music (Ansdell 1995, Nordoff and Robbins 1977). According to of Bruscia (1987), we could consider the balance of words and music in two lights: words *as* music therapy and words *in* music therapy. For Francis words were an expansion of the music – words *in* music therapy. At the end of session eighteen (Chapter 6) he attempted to shed light on the bridge between them. He suggested that poetry could encircle them: '. . . the word is the word and the word partakes of sound, in a sense that it partakes of sound and moves into poetry.' The musical inflections of speech within a free-flowing poetic framework could allow a move between the rationality of words and ethereality of music.

THE ACTIVE LISTENER

The music therapist as active listener was initially introduced in session three (Chapter 3). Later, from session eleven (Chapter 6) onward, my role as listener became established. Francis initiated the term 'active' because he considered my listening to be communicatively reciprocal to his playing. Music therapy is fundamentally based on an alliance between client and therapist, a relationship that is sacrosanct and central to the healing process. Francis acknowledged our relationship as pivotal for his growth. Early on, he had tried to emulate his creative expression outside the sessions, but immediately realized that the growing content of our relationship was a factor that could not be discounted.

155

The literature (Chapter 6) disclosed how little was known about the therapist as listener. Through discussions with other music therapists I began to understand that while the dynamics of listening in therapy were recognized, no one seemed to have knowledge of a therapeutic process in which the therapist was consistently silent. The realigning in my relationship with Francis was simultaneously unsettling and liberating: gradually I learned to understand the importance of the receptive role – not receptive in a passive sense, but as a real and continuing creative part of the music, mute perhaps, but actively resonating.

Subsequent clinical practice, particularly with clients approaching death, has confirmed that it is possible for a therapist to participate fully in music therapy without being musically active. Clients' unaccompanied expression of suffering within music can be simple yet complex. They may realize an intensity of communication that transcends their accustomed standards of musical ability. The therapeutic consequences of producing music that is beyond their normal technical bounds are profound.

My approach now includes both listening to clients' musical outpourings, and improvising for them while they take the role of active listeners. When a therapeutic relationship has been established and a client becomes too ill to play, communication can often continue with him or her in a receptive role. The client's response to a 'musical mirroring' by the music therapist can be uniquely significant. The sense of solitude yet oneness that can arise provides a channel that cuts across consciousness towards the client's inner world. I find that through a poised, attentive 'holding off' and reflecting that allows a client's voice to speak through his or her inactivity, I am able to facilitate music that is a product of us both. This form of inspiritive therapeutic expression, first put forward by Nordoff and Robbins in their work with autistic children (Nordoff and Robbins 1965, 1971), has had far-reaching repercussions in my work. The sense of spirituality pervading a relationship built between musical creator and listener normally evolves during the course of the ongoing therapeutic process; occasionally such an expression of the soul is achieved within one session. The dynamics of either can be liberating for client and therapist.[1]

This concept of music therapy is still shrouded in mystery. It touches on what I believe are the intrinsic spiritual aspects of music and dying, and is approached by Bruscia (1989, pp. 135–1379) in defining music therapy in healing. The duality of expression that can cease in the face of endings, moves toward wholeness through acceptance and receiving stillness. It is difficult to describe these experiences. I owe a great debt to Francis for inaugurating a new area of music therapy endeavour that has continued to flourish. The expertise gained through my experiences with him has had immeasurable effects on my ensuing work in palliative care.

CLOSING COMMENTS

In essence, this book has tried to recapture the feelings of therapist and client during a music therapy process that was based on endings, death and dying. It was my intention to be as honest as possible in what transpired to be an acutely precise therapeutic alliance. Have I been successful in allowing my thoughts to be a vital part of the writing? There were times when I fought the expression of my feelings. Through self-editing these passages would become either diluted or omitted. They were either too painful to see written or too personal to include. There is therefore an underlying sense of objectivity that I initially fought to avoid. Perhaps on reflection it would have been impossible to be totally open, for that in itself would have invalidated the true essence of our relationship.

It is my hope that this book will attract the reader outside the realms of therapy and health-care. I want equally to reach artists and the non-specific readers who have an interest in developing relationships. That people with HIV and AIDS might be encouraged to think about the possibility of music therapy has been a further incentive to keep the writing non-technical. If Francis's verbal and musical explorations in any way relate to and help in other people's life experiences then the completion of this book will have been worthwhile. Francis's legacy to me was that he advocated a way of working that balanced necessary professional detachment, compassion and artistic integrity.

Thinking about Francis some four years after his death, I am reminded of Buber (1937) who says: 'The memory itself is transformed, as it plunges out of its isolation into the unity of the whole.' Has my memory of Francis changed during the writing of this book? I had always believed that after completion I would finally be able to say goodbye. My fantasy had been to climb a hill, look out across the countryside and commemorate the end of our work. I felt a need to mark the end with a definitive full stop. But as the closing words of Chapter 10 express it, 'My relationship with Francis continues'. This being so, it is appropriate that his voice be heard once more, rejoining mine to conclude the book and complete his legacy. He left the following statement to me in his will. Its content suggests that it was written during our work together, probably in the early months, before he became too ill. As he puts forward his views on art, life and the universe, his voice rings with the uncompromising clarity that was authentically his. His thoughts are characteristically incisive and all-inclusive, penetrating yet poetic. All he has to say breathes with the creativity he brought to music therapy. The inclusion of his essay brings back the intensity with which he lived, and adds to the portrayal of my extraordinary colleague, companion in creativity, mentor – and friend.

CODA: ON THE CREATIVE

The visible world is no longer a reality
and the unseen world is no longer a dream.
W. B. Yeats

Art is people being creative, doing everything as well as possible, is emotion recollected in tranquillity, or calculated spontaneity within the cultural values of inherited tradition. Art is awareness of the present overflowing with all time, is the Vision Quest of the Plains Indians, a journey into the experience of all mankind and his archetypes. Art awakens the consciousness proclaiming the psychic unity and underlying brotherhood of creative man, thereby threatening the dominance of established authority.

Reality, since the age of Plato, has waged war on man's fantasy and wholeness. The libidinous realism of Ancient Egypt and Archaic Greek art depicting the universe – not as it appears but as it is, not as the eye sees but as the mind comprehends – was gradually, and until recent times, distorted by the sensory illusion of scientific realism. This is most immediately apparent in the history of European painting, Renaissance perspective, Baroque chiaroscuro, Impressionist colour, Cezanne's peripheral vision and Picasso's breakdown of constant localization. Today, new primitives, new thinkers and artists, bear witness to the re-birth of man's self-organization. Through total communication, non-verbal intercourse in society has moved toward a reorganisation of our imaginative lives. It demands a deep personal involvement and participation, such as required by the conversational immediacy of jazz, the Gebracht Musik of Carl Orff, and Seurat's 'A Sunday Afternoon on the Island of La Grande Jatte'. As objects create their own space and as electricity is the product of certain spatial relationships, so man through the individuality of his aesthetic response may rediscover his soul as the natural extension of his own self-organization. Proclaiming a depth involvement John Cage gives us five minutes of silence (4' 32''), Stockhausen asks us to gather round and contemplate a single note (Stimmung), and at a Paris exhibition we stand and gaze at an empty canvas.

In an ideal society, Plato tells us, art would be subversive; Freud thinks we might well do without it, Maslow talks of its necessity. Is art life or an imitation of life? A balanced acting out of the complex unity of tension and resolution is mirrored in the harmonic and rhythmic possibilities of the Classical Style. Is music an inquiry into a competence with no knowledge of truth, allowed as a diversion – but still undermining the rational ego with disturbing emotions? Does art illuminate, suggest, reveal through the ambiguity of paradox and metaphor, patterns and interplay of experience? Since the eighteenth century, Schiller, Schopenhauer, Bergson and others have questioned rationality and drawn attention to the survival value of art – and that bridge between function and art, biological play. For man is indeed a flexible and adaptive creature, specialist in non-specialization, with an in-built exploratory drive. In song and story, space and time, man makes sense of his life and environment, providing a framework of reference for his awareness of himself and other species. It is a search for synthesis and fulfilment at ever higher levels of perception. Harmony and stability out of discord and chaos, resolved symbolically to grasp the discrepant and thereby make it whole. If architecture is frozen music then creativity is the supreme musical experience, the song of songs which irrefragably state the divine totality and ever present eternal life.

Cooke claims that music is the language of emotion, Meyer devotes an entire volume to the study of 'Emotion and Meaning in Music', Bernstein looks for a universal musical grammar stemming from an innate linguistic and musical competence, while Stravinsky says that music is non-referential, that sounds are meaningless things fashioned into patterns with compelling logic. Hindemith, ignoring the problem of fusing emotion and technique, sets up the doctrine of craft for craft's sake. May we perhaps follow a pattern of ever more diversified articulation in music – from an initial state of energy in vibrating motion, the music of the spheres, the tones of the harmonic series, latent unorganized intervals, through animal calls and bird song – to the linguistic and musical articulation of man crossing the bridge of function-play–art into the realm of symbolic resolution, ambiguous expectancy, and emotional fulfilment? The glimpse into the garden! The realization of the complexity, subtlety and ingeniousness underlying the aesthetic surface structure. The rhythmic balance and harmonic proportions of Mozart's tonal expanses and diatonically contained chromaticism. It is this conceptualization that enables man to contain himself in the discrete elements of his experience.

Then what of the crisis of the twentieth century? The age of protest and despair that has pushed symbolic ambiguity to the edge. What of Tippett holding on to his creative balance by looking straight at his all-pervading grief (Child of Our Time)? Of Nash's Dead Sea? Of Brecht finding unbearable the beauty of trees in a world where those who wished to prepare the ground for friendliness could not be friendly themselves? Of T. Williams with nowhere to go, living in a world without tenderness, extolling nature's peaceful acceptance of decay, his own love of easeful death: 'without a cry, without a prayer / with no betrayal of despair'?

Perhaps a clue may be found in Lewis Carroll's frolicking acceptance of Alice's Wonderland, and Hopkins's (*Pied Beauty*) timely reminder of the deep stability underpinning change: 'All things counter, original, spare, strange; / Whatever is fickle, freckled (who knows how?) / with swift, slow; sweet, sour; adazzle, dim; / He fathers-forth whose beauty is past change: / Praise him.' Life, says Jose Hierro, is body and soul together. Is then the twentieth century the age of the integration of the ultimate paradox-ambiguity? The conscious articulation of the unconscious bringing to a close the long journey that started in the Garden of Eden and the Tower of Babel?

The way in which man can take in his stride the constant enrichment is reflected in the musical development of Western Europe. The perception of single notes leading to the pentatonic scale, extended by addition to six, seven, eight, twelve divisions, quarter tones and microtones, by the constant articulation of the gap. The move from single line to polyphony, the emergence of the third and the sixth – once octaves – fifths and fourths. Bach's codification of the twelve steps, the dramatic potential of tonic–dominant tension through the circle of fifths, realized by Mozart and Haydn. The romantic extension of chromaticism with sevenths and ninths further changing tonal roots and augmented chords with their implicit ambiguity. The continued search to give chords independence on a par with the notes of the scale in Debussy, whose sounds are as evocatively separate as an Egyptian hieroglyphic. All finally bring us to the twelve-tone system of Schoenberg and the new tension of absolute equality wherein tonal order is provided by the surface itself. The idea of composition in this last quarter of the twentieth century is perhaps the total acceptance of the rich intertwining or kaleidoscopic perception of objective and subjective reality. A simultaneity of experience in which tradition is now, and movie-like rolled up like a Roman wall and released as a magic carpet. So Berio unites musical collages reminiscent of a Fellini film, both demanding the integrating presence of individual depth response and coordination. Stockhausen reaffirms the collectivity of equals participating in the act of creation, and jazz today closes the gap between highbrow and lowbrow in a performance that is at once creation and composition in an instant.

Haydn embraced trees and birds and chords in his inspiration. Liszt depicted mountain and stream and the benediction of God. Berlioz showed us the musician in the hallucination of the creative movement. Wagner strove to depict the whole reality and human emotion in a single work of art. Debussy gave us an entire gallery of seascapes, landscapes, woodscapes and portraits, Ravel gave us a menagerie. Janacek studied the rhythm of nature and the law of life. Copland revealed the multiplicity of approach out of time into eternity. Xenakis has welcomed the age of the computer. All this and heaven too is now our heritage, and if reason could not cope with resonance today, then all is allowed. Our unified sensibility may cavort amidst a wider range of awareness which makes ours one of the richest ages of music, poetry, sculpture, painting and architecture alike.

I have at last emerged from my dream. I live.

(Eluard)

'And therefore I have sailed the seas and come to the holy city of Byzantium'

(W. B. Yeats)

NOTES

2 IMPROVISATION, MUSIC THERAPY AND AIDS

1 GIM is 'a technique which involves listening in a relaxed state to selected music, a programmed tape or live music, in order to elicit mental imagery symbols and deep feelings arising from a deeper conscious self' (Bonny 1971). GIM is a potent tool for addressing many of the issues faced by people with HIV and AIDS. In two in-depth studies Bruscia (1991, 1995b) describes the guided imagery process from the perspective of both therapist and client. Bruscia discusses five 'dynamic elements': imagery, music, mandalas, the therapist's personal experiences and the client–therapist relationship. The effectiveness of GIM with clients with HIV and AIDS depends on the maturity of the client and the openness of desired self-healing.

3 CREATIVITY AND CHAOS – ASSESSMENT AND SESSIONS ONE TO FIVE

1 The whole-tone scale is based entirely on tones, i.e. without semitones. It is used periodically by many twentieth-century composers, most notably Debussy (Lester 1989).
2 For a more in-depth discussion on active listening see the opening of Chapter 6 and in Chapter 11.
3 Part of this quotation is included in *Art and Music: Therapy and Research*, eds A. Gilroy and C. Lee (1995), p. 44.

4 WRITTEN ON THE WIND – SESSIONS SIX TO TEN

1 For a more in-depth discussion on active listening see Chapter 11.
2 (a) Part of this quotation is included in *Art and Music: Therapy and Research*, eds A. Gilroy and C. Lee (1995). (b) For audio extracts four and five, see transcribed scores, figures 2 and 3. The music is related to the text by timings notated at the beginning of each bar.
3 Part of this quotation is included in *Art and Music: Therapy and Research*, eds A. Gilroy and C. Lee (1995), p. 45.
4 For further exploration please hear the improvisation from 'Music for Life' Chapter 16 (Charlie), Ansdell (1995). The improvisation from sessions with another client at London Lighthouse (client on guitar, therapist on piano) shows

fundamental aspects of musical expression where the client at times musically supports the therapist.

5 The whole of the improvisation is included on the accompanying CD, giving a sense of a complete musical production. Owing to the length of the extract and complexity of musical construction, the description is more general than in other areas of the book. As discussed in Chapter 1 it is suggested that the listener should not attempt to differentiate between players.

7 SEARCHING FOR THE LIGHT – SESSIONS NINETEEN TO TWENTY-SIX

1 The harmonic shift at the end of this passage was indicative of the unexpected changes in Francis's improvisational style at this time.

11 AFTERWORD

1 This aspect of music therapy will be discussed in more depth in a future publication on spirituality, music and dying.

REFERENCES AND FURTHER
READING

Agawu, V. K. (1991) *Playing with Signs. A Semiotic Interpretation of Classical Music*, Princeton: Princeton University Press.

Aldridge, D. (1989) 'A Phenomenological comparison of the organisation of music and the self', in *The Arts in Psychotherapy* 16, pp. 91–7.

Aldridge, D. and Neugebauer, L. (1990) *Music Therapy and AIDS*, Institute for Music Therapy, Universität Witten/Herdecke.

Alvin, J. (1975) *Music Therapy*, London: Hutchinson.

Ansdell, G. (1995) *Music For Life. Aspects of Creative Music Therapy with Adult Clients*, London and Bristol, Pennsylvania: Jessica Kingsley Publishers.

Bailey, D. (1992) *Improvisation: Its Nature and Practice in Music*, The British Library, National Sound Archive.

Bailey, L. (1983) 'The effects of live music versus tape-recorded music on hospitalised cancer patients', *Music Therapy* 3, pp. 17–28.

Bailey, L. (1984) 'The use of songs in music therapy with cancer patients and their families', *Music Therapy* 4 (1), pp. 5–17.

Bailey, L. (1985) 'The role of music therapy', *Management of Cancer Pain*, New York, Memorial Sloan-Kettering Cancer Centre.

Berendt, J. E. (1985) *The Third Ear. On Listening to the World*, Shaftesbury, Dorset; Rockport, Mass.; Brisbane, Queensland: Element Books.

Bloom, E., ed., (1961) *Grove's Dictionary of Music*, 5th edn, London: Macmillan.

Bonny, H. (1971) *Facilitating GIM Sessions*, Salina, KS: Bonny Foundation.

Bonny, H. (1978) *The Role of Taped Music Programmes in the GIM Process*, Baltimore, MD: ICM Books.

Bright, R. (1986) *Grieving: A Handbook for Those Who Care*, St Louis, MO: Magna Music Baton; London: Schott.

Bruscia, K. (1987) *Improvisational Models of Music Therapy*, Springfield, IL: Charles C. Thomas.

Bruscia, K. (1989) *Defining Music Therapy*, Philadelphia: Barcelona Publishers.

Bruscia, K. (1991) 'Embracing life with AIDS: psychotherapy through guided imagery and music (GIM)', in *Case Studies in Music Therapy* (ed. Bruscia), Philadelphia: Barcelona Publishers.

Bruscia, K. (1995a) 'Images of AIDS', in C. Lee (ed.) *Lonely Waters: Proceedings from the International Conference, Music Therapy in Palliative Care*, Oxford: Sobell House Publications.

Bruscia, K. (1995b) 'Modes of consciousness in guided imagery and music (GIM): a therapist's experience of the guiding process', in C. B. Kenny (ed.) *Listening, Playing, Creating: Essays on the Power of Sound*, New York: State University of New York Press.

Buber, M. (1937) *I and Thou*, Edinburgh: T. and T. Clark.

Bunt, L. (1994) *Music Therapy: An Art Beyond Words*, London and New York: Routledge.

Cage, J. (1968) *Silence*, London: Marion Boyars.

Cantacuzino, M. (1993) *Till Break of Day. Meeting the Challenge of HIV and AIDS at London Lighthouse*, London: Heinemann.

Casement, P. (1985) *On Learning From the Patient*, London and New York: Tavistock Publications.

Cooke, D. (1959) *The Language of Music*, London: Oxford University Press.

Cox, M. (1978) *Structuring the Therapeutic Process*, London: Jessica Kingsley Publishers.

Crocker, D. (1957) 'Music as a therapeutic experience for the emotionally disturbed child', in E. T. Gaston (ed.) *Music Therapy* 7, pp. 114–19.

Dalley, T., Rifkind, G. and Terry, K. (1993) *Three Voices of Art Therapy: Image, Client, Therapist*, London and New York: Routledge.

Dass, R. and Gorman, P. (1985) *How Can I Help?* New York: Alfred A. Knopf.

Dean, R. (1989) *Creative Improvisation: Jazz, Contemporary Music and Beyond*, Milton Keynes: Open University Press.

Delmonte, H. (1995) 'Why work with the dying?', in *Lonely Waters. Proceedings from the International Conference, Music Therapy in Palliative Care*, Oxford: Sobell House Publications.

Durant, D. (1984) 'Improvisation – Arguments after the fact', *The Proceedings of the Forum held at the Institute of Contemporary Arts*, London: The Association of Improvising Musicians, pp. 5–10.

Erdonmez, D. (1993) 'Music. A mega vitamin for the brain', in M. Heal and T. Wigram, eds, *Music Therapy in Health and Education*, London: Jessica Kingsley Publishers.

Fagen, E. T. (1982) 'Music therapy in the treatment of anxiety and fear in terminal patients', *Music Therapy* 2 (1), pp. 13–23.

Forinash, M. (1990) 'Research in music therapy with the terminally ill: a phenomenological approach', DA dissertation, Ann Arbor, University Microfilms 91–02617.

Frank, J. (1985) 'The effects of music therapy and guided visual imagery on chemotherapy-induced nausea and vomiting', *Oncology Nurses Forum* 12 (5), pp. 47–52.

Gilbert, J. (1977) 'Music therapy perspectives on death and dying', *Journal of Music Therapy* 14 (4), pp. 165–71.

Gilroy, A. and Lee, C, eds (1995) *Art and Music: Therapy and Research*, London and New York: Routledge.

Grinell, B. L. (1980) 'The developmental therapeutic process: a new theory of therapeutic intervention', Doctoral dissertation, Bryn Mawr, PA: Bryn Mawr College.

Hartley, N. (1984) 'In retrospect, in prospect. Creative music therapy with those who are living with or who are affected by HIV/AIDS', *International Conference. Music Therapy in Palliative Care*, Oxford: Sir Michael Sobell House.

Hayes, M. (1994) *The Infinite Harmony. Musical Structures in Science and Theology*, London: Weidenfeld & Nicolson.

Heal, M. and Wigram, T., eds (1993) *Music Therapy in Health and Education*, London and Philadelphia: Jessica Kingsley Publishers.

Heimlich, E. P. (1965) 'The specialised use of music as a mode of communication in the treatment of disturbed children', *Journal of the American Academy of Child Psychiatry* 4 (1), pp. 86–122.

Hosinger, T. (1992) *Cello Fever, The Wire* Magazine 96, pp. 18–21.

Johnson-Laird, P. N. (1991) 'Jazz improvisation: a theory at the computational level', in *Representing Musical Structure* (eds P. Howell, R. West and I. Cross), London: Academic Press.

Jung, C. G. (1963) *Memories, Dreams, Reflections*, London and New York: Collins/Routledge & Kegan Paul.

Jung, C. G. (1972) *Four Archetypes. Mother, Rebirth, Spirit, Trickster*, London and New York: Routledge & Kegan Paul.

Kaczynski, T. (1984) *Conversations with Witold Lutoslawski*, London: Chester Music.

Kennedy (1980) *The Concise Oxford Dictionary of Music*, 3rd edn, London: Oxford University Press.

Kerkvliet, G. (1972) 'Music therapy may help control cancer pain', *Journal of the National Cancer Institute* 8882 (5), pp. 350–2.

Lee, C. A. (1989) 'Structural analysis of therapeutic improvisatory music', *Journal of British Music Therapy* 3 (2), pp. 11–19.

Lee, C. A. (1990) 'Structural analysis of post–tonal therapeutic improvisatory music', *Journal of British Music Therapy* 4 (1), pp. 6–20.

Lee, C. A. (1991) 'Foreword: Endings', *Journal of British Music Therapy* 5 (1), pp. 3–4.

Lee, C. A. (1992a) 'The analysis of therapeutic improvisatory music with people living with the virus HIV and AIDS', unpublished PhD thesis, City University, London.

Lee, C. A. (1992b) 'The relationship between music therapy and psychotherapy. The need for professional questioning', *Journal of British Music Therapy* 6 (1).

Lee, C. A. (1995a) 'The analysis of therapeutic improvisatory music', in A. Gilroy and C. Lee (eds) *Art and Music: Therapy and Research*.

Lee, C. A., ed. (1995b) *Lonely Waters, Proceedings from the International Conference, Music Therapy in Palliative Care*, Oxford, Sobell House Publications.

Lester, J. (1989) *Analytic Approaches to Twentieth-Century Music*, London and New York: W. W. Norton & Company.

Levinson, J. (1990) *Music, Art, and Metaphysics. Essays in Philosophical Aesthetics*, London and Ithaca, NY: Cornell University Press.

Lortat-Jacob, B. (1987) *L'improvisation dans les musiques de tradition orale*, Paris, S.E.L.A.F.

Lutoslawski, W. (1988) *Composer's note, Chain 2 Dialogue for violin and orchestra*, London: J. & W. Chester/Editions Wilhelm Hansen.

Magill-Levreault, L. (1993) 'Music therapy in pain and symptom management', *Journal of Palliative Care* 9 (4), pp. 42–8.

Malcolm, N. (1990) *George Enesco. His Life and Music*, London: Toccata Press.

Mandel, S. (1991) 'Music therapy in the hospice: "Musicalive"', *Palliative Medicine* 5, pp. 156–60.

Mandel, S.E. (1993) 'The role of the music therapist on the hospice/palliative care team', *Journal of Palliative Medicine* 9 (4), pp. 37–42.

Martin, J., ed. (1989) 'Music therapy in palliative care. The next step forward. Music therapy with the terminally ill', *Proceedings from a Symposium for Music Therapists' Working in Palliative Care*, New York: Calvary Hospital.

Mathieu, W. A. (1994) *The Musical Life. Reflections on What It Is and How to Live It*, Boston and London: Shambhala Books.

Maya, M. (1992) Quote from *Improvisation in Music. On the Edge*, narrated D. Bailey, Programme Two: Movements in Time, London: Channel Four Television.

Meyer, L. B. (1956) *Emotion and Meaning in Music.* Chicago: University of Chicago Press.

Moranto, C. D. (1993a) 'Applications of music in medicine', in M. Heal and T. Wigram, eds, *Music Therapy in Health and Education*, London and Philadelphia: Jessica Kingsley Publishers.

Moranto, C. D. (1993b) *Music Therapy: International Perspectives*, Piperville, PA: Jeffrey Books.

Munro, S. (1978) 'Music therapy in palliative care', *The Canadian Medical Association Journal* 9, pp. 119, 1029–34.

Munro, S. (1984) *Music Therapy in Palliative/Hospice Care*, St Louis, MO: Magna Music Baton, Inc.

Munro, S. (1988) 'Music therapy in support of cancer patients', in H. J. Senn, A. M. Glaus and L. Schmid, eds, *Recent Results in Cancer Research*, Heidelberg: Springer, 108, pp. 289–94.

Munro, S. (1994) 'Music therapy', *Oxford Textbook of Palliative Medicine*, Oxford: Oxford University Press, pp. 555–9.

Nattiez, J. (1990) *Music and Discourse. Toward a Semiology of Music*, Princeton: Princeton University Press.

Nordoff, P. and Robbins, C. (1965) *Music Therapy for Handicapped Children*, Blauvelt, NY: Rudolf Steiner Publications.

Nordoff, P. and Robbins, C. (1971) *Therapy in Music for Handicapped Children*, London: Gollancz.

Nordoff, P. and Robbins, C. (1977) *Creative Music Therapy*, New York: Harper & Row.

Nuland, S. B. (1994) *How We Die*, London: Chatto & Windus.

O'Callaghan, C. (1984) 'Musical profiles of dying patients', *The Australian Music Therapy Association Bulletin* 7 (2), pp. 5–11.

O'Callaghan, C. (1989) 'Isolation in an isolated spot: Music therapy in palliative care in Australia', in *The Next Step Forward. Music therapy with the terminally ill. Proceedings from a symposium for music therapists working in palliative care*, New York: Calvary Hospital, pp. 33–44.

O'Callaghan, C. (1990) 'Music therapy skills used in songwriting within a palliative care setting', *The Australian Journal of Music Therapy* 1, pp. 15–22.

O'Callaghan, C. (1993) 'Communicating with brain-impaired palliative care patients through music therapy', *Journal of Palliative Care* 9 (4), pp. 53–5.

Oldfield, A. (1993) 'A study of the way music therapists analyse their work', *Journal of British Music Therapy* 7 (1), pp. 14–22.

Osmond-Smith, D. (1985) *Playing on Words, A Guide to Luciano Berio's Sinfonia*, London: Royal Musical Association.

Pavlicevic, M. (1991) 'Music in communication: improvisation in music therapy', unpublished PhD thesis, University of Edinburgh.

Payne, H., ed. (1993) *Handbook of Inquiry in the Arts Therapies. One River, Many Currents*, London and Philadelphia: Jessica Kingsley Publishers.

Pressing, J. (1984) 'Improvisation', in *Cognitive Processes in the Perception of Art*, eds W. A. Crozier and A. J. Chapman, Amsterdam: Elsevier Science Publications.

Prevost, E. (1984) 'Commentary on the proceedings', in *The Proceedings of the Forum Held at the Institute of Contemporary Arts*, London: Association of Improvising Musicians.

Priestley, M. (1975) *Music Therapy in Action*, St Louis, MO: Magna Music Baton.

Priestley, M. (1994) *Essays on Analytic Music Therapy*, Philadelphia: Barcelona Publishers.

Reason, P. and Rowan, J., eds (1981) *Human Inquiry. A Sourcebook of New Paradigm Research*, Chichester, New York, Brisbane, Toronto: John Wiley & Sons.

Rinpoche, S. (1992) *The Tibetan Book of Living and Dying*, London and San Francisco: Rider Books.

Robbins, C. (1993) 'The creative processes are universal', in *Music Therapy in Health and Education*, eds M. Heal and T. Wigram, London and Bristol, Pennsylvania: Jessica Kingsley Publishers.

Salmon, D. (1993) 'Music and emotion in palliative care', *Journal of Palliative Medicine* 9 (4), pp. 48–52.

Samson, J. (1977) *Music in Transition. A Study of Tonal Expansion and Atonality, 1900–1920*, London: J. M. Dent.

Scheiby, B. (1991) 'Mia's Fourteenth – The Symphony of Fate: psychodynamic improvisation therapy with a music therapy student in training', in K. Bruscia, ed., *Case Studies in Music Therapy*, Philadelphia: Barcelona Publishers.

Schopenhauer, A. (1819) *The World as Will and Idea*, trans. R. B. Haldane and J. Kemp, 4th edn, 3 vols, London: Kegan Paul, Trench and Trübner (1896).

Scott (1934) *Beethoven*.

Schroeder-Sheker, T. (1993) 'Music for the dying: the new field of music thanatology', *Advances* 9 (1).

Shilts, R. (1987) *And the Band Played On. Politics, People and the AIDS Epidemic*, New York: St Martins Press.

Short, P. (1993) Review of 'Music Therapy in Health and Education', eds M. Heal and T. Wigram, *Journal of British Music Therapy* 7 (2), pp. 28–30.

Sobell Publications (1991) *Mud and Stars. The Impact of Hospice Experience on the Church's Ministry of Healing*, Oxford: Sobell Publications.

Solomon, L. (1986) 'Improvisation 2, Perspectives', *New Music* 24, pp. 224–35.

Sondheim, S. (1984) *Sunday in the Park with George*, New York: Revelation Music Publishing Corporation and Rilting Music, Inc.

Spitz, E. H. (1985) *Art and Psyche. A Study in Psychoanalysis and Aesthetics*, New Haven and London: Yale University Press.

Steele, P. (1988) Foreword, *Journal of British Music Therapy* 2 (2).

Storr, A. (1992) *Music and the Mind*, London and New York: Harper Collins.

Tippett, M. (1980) *Music of the Angels*, London: Eulenberg Books.

Tweedie, I. (1979) *The Chasm of Fire*, Shaftesbury, Dorset; Rockport, MA; Brisbane, Queensland: Element Books.

Watson, O., ed. (1976) *Longman's Modern English Dictionary*, 2nd edn, Harlow: Longman.

Wigram, T. (1993) 'Observational techniques in the analysis of both active and receptive music therapy with disturbed and self-injurious clients', in *Music Therapy in Health and Education*, eds M. Heal and T. Wigram, London and Philadelphia: Jessica Kingsley Publishers.

Wilson, C. (1964) *Brandy of the Damned*.

Winarski, M. (1991) *AIDS Related Psychotherapy*, Oxford: Pergamon General Psychology.

Whittal, J. (1990) *A Handbook of Music Therapy in Palliative/Hospice Care*, Montreal: Palliative Care Service, Royal Victoria Hospital.

Whittal, J. (1991) 'Songs in palliative care: A spouse's last gift', in K. Bruscia, ed., *Case Studies in Music Therapy*, Philadelphia: Barcelona Publishers, pp. 603–10.

Zinn, D. (1981) *The Structure and Analysis of the Modern Improvised Line*, New York: Excelsior Music Publishing Company.

INDEX

TRACK LISTING

Mastering by Nick Watson at Sound Recording Technology.

The CD is comprised of improvisations made during actual therapy sessions. Due to the fact that recording levels varied, a small amount of distortion may at times have occurred.